New Frontiers in Translation Studies

Empirical Translation Modelling

Empirical translation has become a mainstream research branch in translation studies in recent years with the rise of empiricism in the humanities and the social sciences in Europe at the turn of the twenty-first century. It is an interdisciplinary, methodologically oriented research paradigm which seeks to explore language and textual patterns in translations in relation to the source language and texts or the original target language. Language corpora or digital text collections provide the essential research resources for empirical translation. As a result, empirical translation and corpus translation have been used as largely exchangeable concepts. With the increasing availability of large quantities of web-based natural language and translation resources, there is a growing trend to introduce data science methods to empirical translation research, which has been mainly using statistics to explore linguistic and textual patterns in translations. This new Springer Briefs series will usher in a new period of disciplinary development in empirical translation studies by introducing data science methods and techniques in the study of a wide range of translation genres, products, services, and social activities. Empirical translation modelling refers to both the statistical and computational modelling of translations and related language and text materials, as well as related societal and human behavioural patterns and events. This new series aims to provoke academic debates among scholars of translation studies and cognate fields such as linguistics, computer science, natural language processing, statistics the feasibility and productivity of using statistics and machine learning methods to advance translation research ranging from translation quality assessment, translation technology evaluation to healthcare and health risk translation and communication, and global policy translation such as social and environmental sustainability and social equality. This new series is visionary and pioneering for both its focus on research methodological innovation and the broader research agenda it aims to develop for empirical translation studies. Titles in this series will illustrate important social, environmental contributions that empirical translation research can and will make to more sustainable and equitable social development around the world.

Yi Shan · Meng Ji

Chinese Mental Health Scale Translation

Springer

Yi Shan
School of Foreign Studies
Nantong University
Nantong, China

Meng Ji
School of Languages and Cultures
The University of Sydney
Sydney, Australia

ISSN 2197-8689 ISSN 2197-8697 (electronic)
New Frontiers in Translation Studies
ISSN 2731-0515 ISSN 2731-0523 (electronic)
SpringerBriefs in Empirical Translation Modelling
ISBN 978-981-97-2268-6 ISBN 978-981-97-2269-3 (eBook)
https://doi.org/10.1007/978-981-97-2269-3

© The Author(s) 2024. This book is an open access publication.

Open Access This book is licensed under the terms of the Creative Commons Attribution-NonCommercial-NoDerivatives 4.0 International License (http://creativecommons.org/licenses/by-nc-nd/4.0/), which permits any noncommercial use, sharing, distribution and reproduction in any medium or format, as long as you give appropriate credit to the original author(s) and the source, provide a link to the Creative Commons license and indicate if you modified the licensed material. You do not have permission under this license to share adapted material derived from this book or parts of it.

The images or other third party material in this book are included in the book's Creative Commons license, unless indicated otherwise in a credit line to the material. If material is not included in the book's Creative Commons license and your intended use is not permitted by statutory regulation or exceeds the permitted use, you will need to obtain permission directly from the copyright holder.

This work is subject to copyright. All commercial rights are reserved by the author(s), whether the whole or part of the material is concerned, specifically the rights of translation, reprinting, reuse of illustrations, recitation, broadcasting, reproduction on microfilms or in any other physical way, and transmission or information storage and retrieval, electronic adaptation, computer software, or by similar or dissimilar methodology now known or hereafter developed. Regarding these commercial rights a non-exclusive license has been granted to the publisher.

The use of general descriptive names, registered names, trademarks, service marks, etc. in this publication does not imply, even in the absence of a specific statement, that such names are exempt from the relevant protective laws and regulations and therefore free for general use.

The publisher, the authors and the editors are safe to assume that the advice and information in this book are believed to be true and accurate at the date of publication. Neither the publisher nor the authors or the editors give a warranty, expressed or implied, with respect to the material contained herein or for any errors or omissions that may have been made. The publisher remains neutral with regard to jurisdictional claims in published maps and institutional affiliations.

This Springer imprint is published by the registered company Springer Nature Singapore Pte Ltd.
The registered company address is: 152 Beach Road, #21-01/04 Gateway East, Singapore 189721, Singapore

If disposing of this product, please recycle the paper.

Preface

The unfolding pandemic in the twenty-first century reopened debates on how to communicate diseases without causing harms. Every disease, through interaction with humans, has developed its own socio-psychological properties in different cultures. Some can cause tremendous fears and anxiety like cancer and some can cause guilt, shame, isolation, like HIV/AIDS and dementia. The pandemic illustrates that stigma can cause harms in many ways to people infected with the disease. Disease stigmatisation is connived in many cultures and is ongoing with many diseases that we lack knowledge of, affecting more concentrated, vulnerable populations like elderly people with dementia.

Stigmatising language can be a stumbling block to treatment and support and increase the likelihood of dementia worsening before treatment is instituted. Unfortunately, stigmatisation of dementia is rooted in many cultures. For example, in multicultural Australia, the prevalence of dementia is higher among English-speaking people (8.8%) than those with Chinese (4.9%), Vietnamese (4.8%), Arabic (4.6%) cultural backgrounds, reflecting decreasing openness, willingness to report, and diagnose dementia, due to concerns of stigma within cultural communities despite stigma is a universal experience, it can manifest differently across cultural and language contexts.

Research has found that inclusive language in English is highly effective to help destigmatise mental health conditions. Based on similar research evidence supporting inclusive language reforms, mental health research and promotion organisations such as Dementia Australia released the national guidelines of inclusive language for dementia care and aged care. Inclusive terms like 'impact of supporting people with dementia', 'changed behaviours', 'condition', 'stressful' were proposed to replace discriminatory words like 'carer burden' 'unbearable' 'difficult behaviours', 'illness', 'devastating', etc. In multicultural English-speaking countries, translation from English to migrant languages serves as a major source of health knowledge for multicultural Australians. Despite the availability of new guidelines of inclusive English language use in mental health, it remains unknown whether and how new English language guidelines can be translated, effectively, to community languages and cultures that are distinctively different from English.

In this book, we discuss some key steps and procedures of translating mental health scales into linguistically and culturally appropriate translations in Mandarin Chinese. Through illustrative case studies, we demonstrate that traditional forward and backward translation have significant methodological limitations when applied in mental health scale translation, such as linguistic and cultural inaccessibility and inaccuracy in the clinic. We wish our book will stimulate more academic debates and further systematic research into the significant, interdisciplinary area of mental health scale translations in translation studies.

Sydney, Australia Meng Ji
Shanghai, China Yi Shan
September 2023

Contents

1 **Pressing Need for Chinese Translation of Mental Health Scales** 1
   1.1 Variations in How Mental Disorders Are Expressed 1
   1.2 Pressing Need to Translate and Cross-culturally Adapt Mental Health Scales 3
   1.3 Prevalence of Mental Disorders in China and Translation of Mental Health Scales into Chinese 5
   References 6

2 **Exemplification of Mental Health Scales** 9
   2.1 Mental Health Scales 9
   2.2 Mental Health Locus of Control Scales 10
   2.3 Attitude Assessment Scales 12
   2.4 Summary 14
   References 14

3 **Translating and Adapting the Multidimensional Health Locus of Control Scale FORM C to a Chinese Scale Specifically Used for Measuring People's Beliefs About the Prevention and Treatment of Depression in Mainland China** 17
   3.1 Background 17
   3.2 Methods 21
      3.2.1 Translation and Adaptation of the MHLC Form C 21
      3.2.2 Using the Chinese MHLC Form C to Classify Patients and Identifying Factors Associated with Low Self-efficacy 23
   3.3 Results 26
      3.3.1 Translation and Adaptation of the MHLC Form C 26
      3.3.2 Using the Chinese MHLC Form C to Classify Patients and Identifying Factors Associated with Low Self-efficacy 37
   3.4 Discussion 55
      3.4.1 Principal Findings 55

		3.4.2	Implications	57
		3.4.3	Limitations	58
		3.4.4	Conclusions	58
	References			59
4	**Development of a Method and an Assessment Construct for Person-Centered Translation of Dementia Public Stigma Scales**			**63**
	4.1	Introduction		64
		4.1.1	Prevalence of Dementia and Dementia-Related Stigma	64
		4.1.2	Stigma as a Social Construct	64
		4.1.3	Developing Socioculturally-Relevant Dementia Public Stigma Scales	65
	4.2	Design and Methods		68
		4.2.1	Overall Design	68
		4.2.2	Developing the Chinese Version of the DPSS	69
		4.2.3	Developing a Method and an Assessment Construct for Person-Centered Translation of Dementia Public Stigma Scales	69
	4.3	Results		70
		4.3.1	Mistranslations Arising from the Literal Translation	70
		4.3.2	Root Causes of Mistranslations, Implications for Translation, and Consequences of Forced Literal Translations	70
		4.3.3	An Assessment Construct for Person-Centered Translation of Dementia Public Stigma Scales Proposed	73
		4.3.4	Identification of the Best Translation Among Various Translation Options	74
	4.4	Discussion		76
	References			80

Chapter 1
Pressing Need for Chinese Translation of Mental Health Scales

Abstract People from different cultural backgrounds express mental disorders diversely. Investigating mental health disorders in different cultures is controversial and can best be explained by two positions embedded in cross-cultural psychiatry: the universalistic position versus the relativistic position. Culture can play a significant role in variations in behaviour, and measurement of behavior in a cross-cultural context calls for the use of adapted instruments. The global population (cultural) diversity entails a pressing need for cross-culturally validated measures or scales which can be used to ascertain the varying mental health needs of diverse populations from multicultural societies. Given the high prevalence of mental disorders and the lack of mental health scales in China, it is necessary to translate and cross-culturally adapt mental health scales to Chinese.

Keywords Cultural backgrounds · Variations · Mental disorders · Pressing need · Mental health scales · Translation · Cross-cultural adaptation

1.1 Variations in How Mental Disorders Are Expressed

As is shown by large-scale epidemiological studies, mental disorders are prevalent in diverse societies and cultures (Flaherty et al., 1988). However, different global prevalence rates of major mental disorders imply that there are variations in how these disorders are expressed (Flaherty, 1988; Draguns & Tanaka-Matsumi, 2003). These variations may partly be explained by the fact that people living in diverse social contexts experience and communicate emotional distress in different ways (Ballenger et al., 2001). As such, psychiatric disorders can be seen as cultural conventions, which mainly define appropriate forms and expressions of suffering (Kirmayer, 2002), resulting in largely variable manifestations, diverse presentations and unique illness categories across cultural settings (Desjarlais et al., 1995; Kirmayer, 2007). For example, Kirmayer (2002) has identified several different forms of mental illness specific to particular cultural settings that are expressed by means of idioms of distress.

Investigating mental health disorders in different cultures is controversial and can best be explained by two positions embedded in cross-cultural psychiatry: the universalistic position versus the relativistic position (Smit et al., 2006). The former holds that emotions result from neurophysiologic processes in the limbic system and are thus biological phenomena, and that there is a limited repertoire of universal emotional experiences (Panksepp, 1998). Advocated in biomedicine, this position highlights categorizing and labeling syndromes (Kleinman & Good, 1985). By contrast, the relativist position argues that emotional expression is socially constructed and thus specific to a given historical, societal and cultural system (Lutz, 1985). Held by ethnographic and anthropological studies, this position asserts that tools developed in one cultural setting may fail to capture the idiosyncratic ways that emotional distress is expressed in other cultural settings because the context within which people from other cultures live and experience the world may be ignored (Kleinman & Good, 1985).

Both positions have been criticized for their limitations. The universalistic position runs the risk of being imperialistic because it ignores cultural differences and insists on using concepts developed in a Western context as a blueprint for perceiving other cultures (Kleinman & Good, 1985). The relativistic position risks concretizing dissimilarities by ignoring the impacts of acculturation and cultural assimilation (Swartz, 1998), therefore revealing little about similarities (Kirmayer, 2001).

The relativistic position and the universalistic position align respectively with the *emic* and *etic* approaches, two traditional methods of observation adopted in cross-cultural research (Flaherty et al., 1988). These orientations are concerned with the origin of concepts in question (Draguns & Tanaka-Matsumi, 2003; Kinzie & Manson, 1987). As "an insider's view of culture," the emic approach, comparable to the relativistic position, aims at the description of the language and customs of the culture at a specific time by using "culturally defined, within-group independent and dependent (outcome) variables" to gain a granular understanding of concepts relevant to one cultural setting but possibly irrelevant to other cultural settings (Flaherty et al., 1988: 257). This approach can enable us to give a fine-grained description of behaviors within a particular culture at a given time, allowing for descriptively comparing particular phenomena between two cultures and theories to explain observed phenomena. In contrast, within the paradigm of the etic approach, comparable to the universalistic position, the concept of a behavior and techniques for measuring this behavior in one culture is applied to another culture, shedding little light on cultural disparities in the purpose and meaning of behavior (Flaherty et al., 1988). As a result, signs and symptoms of a prevalent disorder (i.e., depression) specific to a particular culture will be overlooked if diagnostic criteria established in a specific Western culture is applied to a non-Western cultural context (Kleinman, 1977). In brief, the emic approach focuses on the meaning that a specific cultural group attaches to a particular notion while the etic approach focuses on the description of phenomena that is independent of meaning (Kinzie & Manson, 1987).

In the final analysis, the nature of emic and etic approaches could largely be revealed by Murphy's (1969) claim that culture enters psychiatric inquiry in two ways: as a distortion and as an object of research. Specifically, the emic approach is adopted when one aims to compare the symptoms of commonly occurring syndromes, such as depression, cross-culturally; on the other hand, the etic approach is used when one seeks to identify the impact of acculturation on depressive symptoms across two particular cultures, and the objective of this approach is to minimize the distortion by culture to make cross-cultural comparisons meaningful (Flaherty et al., 1988).

Attempts have been made to integrate the relativistic and universalistic positions through combining the emic and etic approaches (Smit et al., 2006), with concepts and descriptions that are derived from anthropological studies (an emic orientation) being incorporated into measuring scales, an etic orientation (Draguns & Tanaka-Matsumi, 2003). Such integration finds its full expression in the process in which cultural equivalence is established through the cross-cultural adaptation of psychiatric research instruments (Smit et al., 2006).

In the context of a growing number of populations who could benefit from mental health materials written in their native language, it is necessary to determine an approach to language translation that prioritizes the world view of the target readers (Black, 2018). Such an approach is most likely to identify the variations in how mental disorders are expressed in the target language and cultural settings.

1.2 Pressing Need to Translate and Cross-culturally Adapt Mental Health Scales

Translation is essentially a multilingual and multicultural endeavor that can provide far-reaching implications for the growth and development of the mental health domain worldwide (Black, 2018). Culture can play a substantial role in variations in behaviour, and measurement of behavior in a cross-cultural context calls for the use of adapted instruments (Herdman et al., 1997). The global population (cultural) diversity entails a pressing need for cross-culturally validated measures or scales (Sousa & Rojjanasrirat, 2011), which can be used to ascertain the varying mental health needs of diverse populations from multicultural societies. This need necessitates the translation and cross-cultural adaptation of mental health scales. "Translation, adaptation and validation of an instrument or scale for cross-cultural research is time-consuming and requires careful planning and adoption of rigorous methodological approaches to derive a reliable and valid measure of the concept of interest in the target population." (Sousa & Rojjanasrirat, 2011) Mental health materials thus translated, adapted and validated are most likely to identify the variations in how mental health disorders are expressed in diverse language and cultural settings and therefore capture the varying health needs of multicultural populations across national boundaries and within multicultural communities. To facilitate comparability and deliver appropriate interventions, the best way to identify and assess mental disorders is likely to be an integration of adapting Western instruments (van Ommeren et al., 1999), exploring additional symptoms and expressions that would not be captured through an adaptation-only approach (Kohrt & Hruschka, 2010) and investigating far-reaching influences, including function impairment (Bolton & Tang, 2002).

When reviewing the literature on and proposing guidelines for cross-cultural adaptation of health-related quality of life measures, Guillemin et al. (1993: 1417) observes that "With a few exceptions, all the measures so far developed are in the English language and are intended for use in English-speaking countries." This is also true for other health-related materials, including various instruments like mental health scales. It is, therefore, necessary to have materials available in languages other than English for comprehensive and accurate cross-cultural research, assessment, and education (Johnson & Cameron, 2001; Miranda et al., 2002) in non-English-speaking countries and among a growing number of immigrants in English-speaking communities. Such necessity confirms the settings for cross-cultural adaptation of scales identified by Guillemin et al. (1993). The degree of adaptation depends on similarities and disparities between the languages and cultures of the populations concerned (Brislin et al., 1973). Immigrants recently settled in a host culture may have a low level of acculturation and thus need a measure that is cross-culturally adapted to their native language and culture. For example, immigrants living in America or Australia may encounter specific problems in communicating their needs in English with regard to health-related issues, and they may also assess their health status and perceive health materials of various types based on their language and cultural origin and the degree of being assimilated into the host language and culture. Besides, a scale to be administered in a country other than that where it has been developed may necessitate cross-cultural adaptation since different cultural beliefs have been imprinted in the mind of the people concerned, who are accustomed to referring to their native culture when assessing their health conditions and understanding health materials.

A wide range of English health-related measures have been developed and validated to administer various health-related assessment, screening, interventions, and education. "There is nonetheless a need for measures specifically designed to be used in non-English-speaking countries and also among immigrant populations, since cultural groups vary in disease expression and in their use of various health care systems." (Guillemin et al., 1993: 1417). To meet this need, two approaches can be adopted: developing new tools and using tools already developed in another language. Developing new scales is time-consuming (Shan et al., 2023), with the bulk of the effort made to conceptualize the scale and select and reduce its items (Guillemin et al., 1993). When previously developed measures are transposed through simple translation from their source cultural settings to target cultural contexts, they are most unlikely to be successful due to language and cultural differences (Berkanovic, 1980) and to cultural variations in the perception of particular concepts and constructs and the ways that health issues are expressed (Kleinman et al., 1978). Success in this approach calls for a systematic toolkit that can entail the effective cross-cultural adaptation of original English measures.

Cross-cultural adaptation consists of two essential components: the translation of the measures under investigation and its adaptation. It requires "a combination of the literal translation of individual words and sentences from one language to another and an adaptation with regard to idiom, and to cultural context and lifestyle" (Guillemin et al., 1993: 1421). The quality of an adapted instrument is then subjected to assessment with regard to its sensibility, the essential elements of which include the designed purpose, comprehensibility, content and face validity, replicability and suitability of the scale studied (Feinstein, 1987).

The individuals' perceptions of the scales studied and the ways that health problems are expressed, and health situations are assessed vary from culture to culture (Guillemin et al., 1993; Kleinman et al., 1978). As a result, translating and adapting previously developed instruments cross-culturally may most likely accommodate the varying needs of the populations studied in the target language and culture. This is particularly true for the cross-cultural translation and adaptation of already developed mental health scales, given the growing global prevalence and magnitude of mental health disorders and the resulting burdens on and negative outcomes for the individual and society. Trans-culturally adapting and validating previously developed instruments can facilitate communicating research findings to international audiences who are likely to fund mental health service development (Kohrt et al., 2011). Besides, adapting standardized measures for depression and anxiety can be beneficial regarding administering treatment approaches tailored to such disorders (WHO, 2008). Filling the written language gap in mental health through translation and adaptation not merely helps increase the availability of multi-language written materials, but also helps open educational opportunities that are conventionally delivered through psychoeducation, parenting, preparedness workshops or other oral means (Black, 2018). Additionally, culturally and linguistically appropriate written educational materials promise not only to offer essential information, but also to reduce stigma socially attached to mental health concerns and relevant help-seeking (Black, 2018).

1.3 Prevalence of Mental Disorders in China and Translation of Mental Health Scales into Chinese

In the early 2000s, approximately 17% of adults in China were found to have a mental disorder (Phillips et al., 2009), making China one of the most mentally ill countries worldwide (Demyttenaere et al., 2004). As many as 92% of individuals with mental disorders in China had never sought any type of professional help for their disorder (Phillips et al., 2009). In this background, it is necessary to use scales to assess people's beliefs about, attitudes towards, and knowledge and literacy about mental disorders and to rate and screen mental disorders. However, such scales are very few in China. Therefore, there is a pressing need for the Chinese translation of mental health scales developed in other languages to conduct tailor-made assessment, screening, education, intervention, prevention and treatment in mainland China and possibly in Chinese-speaking communities worldwide.

References

Ballenger, J. C., Davidson, J. R., Lecrubier, Y., Nutt, D. J., Kirmayer, L. J., Lepine, J. P., et al. (2001). Consensus statement on transcultural issues in depression and anxiety from the International Consensus Group on Depression and Anxiety. *Journal of Clinical Psychiatry, 62*(Suppl 13), 47–55.

Berkanovic, E. (1980). The effect of inadequate language translation on Hispanics' responses to health surveys. *American Journal of Public Health, 70*, 1273–1276.

Black, A. K. (2018). *Language translation for mental health materials: A comparison of current back-translation and Skopostheorie-based methods*. All Theses and Dissertations. 6720.

Bolton, P., & Tang, A. (2002). An alternative approach to cross-cultural function assessment. *Social Psychiatry and Psychiatric Epidemiology, 37*(11), 537–543.

Brislin, R. W., Lonner, W. J., & Thorndike, R. M. (1973). Questionnaire wording and translation. *Cross-cultural research methods* (pp. 32–58). John Wiley.

Demyttenaere, K., Bruffaerts, R., Posada-Villa, J., et al. (2004). Prevalence, severity, and unmet need for treatment of mental disorders in the World Health Organization World Mental Health Surveys. *JAMA, 291*, 2581–2590.

Desjarlais, R., Eisenberg, L., Good, B., & Kleinman, A. (1995). *World mental health: Problems and priorities in low-income countries*. Oxford University Press.

Draguns, J. G., & Tanaka-Matsumi, J. (2003). Assessment of psychopathology across and within cultures: Issues and findings. *Behaviour Research and Therapy, 41*(7), 755–776.

Feinstein, A. R. (1987). The theory and evaluation of sensibility. In A. R. Feinstein (Ed.), *Clinimetrics* (pp. 141–166). Yale University Press.

Flaherty, J. A., Gaviria, F. M., Pathak, D., Mitchell, T., Wintrob, R., Richman, J. A., et al. (1988). Developing instruments for cross-cultural psychiatric research. *Journal of Nervous Mental and Disorders, 176*(5), 257–263.

Guillemin, F., Bombardier, C., & Beaton, D. (1993). Cross-cultural adaptation of health-related quality of life measure: Literature review and proposed guidelines. *Journal of Clinical Epidemiology, 46*(12), 1417–1432.

Herdman, M., Fox-Rushby, J., & Badia, X. (1997). "Equivalence" and the translation and adaptation of health-related quality of life questionnaires. *Quality of Life Research, 6*, 237–247.

Johnson, J. L., & Cameron, M. C. (2001). Barriers to providing effective mental health services to American Indians. *Mental Health Services Research, 3*(4), 215–223.

Kirmayer, L. J. (2001). Cultural variations in the clinical presentation of depression and anxiety: Implications for diagnosis and treatment. *Journal of Clinical Psychiatry, 62*(Suppl 13), 22–28.

Kirmayer, L. J. (2002). Psychopharmacology in a globalizing world: The use of antidepressants in Japan. *Transcultural Psychiatry, 39*(3), 295–322.

Kirmayer, L. J. (2007). Psychotherapy and the cultural concept of the person. *Transcultural Psychiatry, 44*(2), 232–257.

Kinzie, J. D., & Manson, S. M. (1987). The use of self-rating scales in crosscultural psychiatry. *Hospital and Community Psychiatry, 38*(2), 190–196.

Kleinman, A. M. (1977). Depression, somatization and the "new cross-cultural psychiatry." *Social Science and Medicine, 11*, 3–10.

Kleinman, A., Eisenberg, L., & Good, B. (1978). Culture, illness and care: Clinical lessons from anthropologic and cross-cultural research. *Annals Internal Medicine, 88*, 251–258.

Kleinman, A. M., & Good, B. (1985). Introduction: Culture and depression. In A. Kleinman & B. Good (Eds.), *Culture and depression: Studies in the anthropology and cross-cultural psychiatry of affect and disorder* (pp. 1–33). University of California Press.

Kohrt, B. A., & Hruschka, D. J. (2010). Nepali concepts of psychological trauma: The role of idioms of distress, ethnopsychology and ethnophysiology in alleviating suffering and preventing stigma. *Culture, Medicine, and Psychiatry, 34*(2), 322–352.

Kohrt, B. A., Jordans, M., Tol, W., Luitel, N., Maharjan, S., & Upadhaya, N. (2011). Validation of cross-cultural child mental health and psychosocial research instruments: Adapting the

References

depression self-rating scale and child PTSD symptom scale in Nepal. *BMC Psychiatry, 11*, 127–143.

Lutz, C. (1985). Depression and the translation of emotional worlds. In A. Kleinman & B. Good (Eds.), *Culture and depression: Studies in the anthropology and cross-cultural psychiatry of affect and disorder* (pp. 63–100). University of California Press.

Miranda, J., Lawson, W., & Escobar, J. (2002). Ethnic minorities. *Mental Health Services Research, 4*(4), 231–237.

Murphy, H.B.M. (1969). Handling the cultural dimension in psychiatric research. *Social Psychiatry, 4*, 11–15.

Panksepp, J. (1998). *The foundations of human and animal emotions*. Oxford University Press.

Phillips, M. R., Zhang, J., Shi, Q., et al. (2009). Prevalence, treatment, and associated disability of mental disorders in four provinces in China during 2001–05: An epidemiological survey. *Lancet, 373*, 2041–2053.

Shan, Y., Ji, M., Dong, Z., Xing, Z., Wang, D., & Cao, X. (2023). The Chinese version of the patient education materials assessment tool for printable materials: Translation, adaptation, and validation study. *Journal of Medical Internet Research, 25*, e39808.

Smit, J., van den Berg, C. E., Bekker, L.-G., Seedat, S., & Stein, D. J. (2006). Translation and cross-cultural adaptation of a mental health battery in an African setting. *African Health Sciences, 6*(4), 215–222.

Sousa, V. D., & Rojjanasrirat, W. (2011). Translation, adaptation and validation of instruments or scales for use in cross-cultural health care research: A clear and user-friendly guideline. *Journal of Evaluation in Clinical Practice, 17*, 268–274.

Swartz, L. (1998). *Culture and mental health: A southern Africa review*. Oxford University Press.

Van Ommeren, M., Sharma, B., Thapa, S., Makaju, R., Prasain, D., Bhattarai, R., & de Jong, J. (1999). Preparing instruments for transcultural research: use of the translation monitoring form with Nepali-speaking Bhutanese Refugees. *Transcultural Psychiatry, 36*(3): 285–301.

World Health Organization (WHO). (2008). *Mental health gap action programme (mhGAP): Scaling up care for mental, neurological and substance abuse disorders*. WHO.

Open Access This chapter is licensed under the terms of the Creative Commons Attribution-NonCommercial-NoDerivatives 4.0 International License (http://creativecommons.org/licenses/by-nc-nd/4.0/), which permits any noncommercial use, sharing, distribution and reproduction in any medium or format, as long as you give appropriate credit to the original author(s) and the source, provide a link to the Creative Commons license and indicate if you modified the licensed material. You do not have permission under this license to share adapted material derived from this chapter or parts of it.

The images or other third party material in this chapter are included in the chapter's Creative Commons license, unless indicated otherwise in a credit line to the material. If material is not included in the chapter's Creative Commons license and your intended use is not permitted by statutory regulation or exceeds the permitted use, you will need to obtain permission directly from the copyright holder.

Chapter 2
Exemplification of Mental Health Scales

Abstract The chapter exemplifies mental health scales with (1) the Multidimensional Health Locus of Control (MHLC) Form C which has been made depression-specific and (2) the Dementia Public Stigma Scale (DPSS).

Keywords Mental health scales · Health locus of control · Attitude assessment tools

2.1 Mental Health Scales

"Mental health problems are a growing public health concern." (Mental Health Foundation, 2016) "Nearly one billion people worldwide suffer from some form of mental disorder, according to latest UN data–a staggering figure that is even more worrying, if you consider that it includes around one in seven teenagers." (UN News, 2022) A recent index of 301 diseases discovered that mental health issues ranked among the major causes of the global overall disease burden (Vos et al., 2013). It has been estimated that 35–50% of individuals living with severe mental health issues in developed countries, and 76–85% in developing countries, receive no treatment (Demyttenaere et al., 2004).

Given the worldwide prevalence of mental health issues and the imbalance between the global disease burden caused by mental health issues and attention paid to these conditions, various types of mental health-related scales have been developed and validated to serve different purposes. These scales can roughly be grouped under four broad headings: (1) mental health locus of control scales; (2) attitude assessment tools; (3) knowledge and literacy scales; and (4) psychiatric rating scales. In the following sections, we will focus on and exemplify the first two categories.

2.2 Mental Health Locus of Control Scales

Since their advent in the mid-late 1970's, the Multidimensional Health Locus of Control (MHLC) Scales Forms A and B have been in use as the "general" health locus of control scales (Wallston, 2023) and remained "one of the most frequently used measures of health-related beliefs" (Wallston et al., 1994). Both forms comprise three 6-item subscales: internality; powerful others externality; and chance externality. They have been used in more than a thousand studies and cited in literature hundreds of times in the past 30 years (Wallston, 2023).

Health locus of control refers to a person's belief regarding where control over his/her health lies (Wallston et al., 1994). "It the person believes that his/her own behavior influences his/her health status, the person is said to possess an *internal* locus of control orientation with regard to his/her health. If, on the other hand, the person believes that his/her health status is influenced by the actions of other people or is due to fate, luck, or chance, the person is said to have an *external* health locus of control orientation." (Wallston et al., 1994: 534) A person's health locus of control orientation is one of several factors that determine his/her health-related behaviors, which, in turn, partially determine his/her health condition (Wallston et al., 1994).

Drawing on Wallston et al. (1994), we can say that mental health locus of control means a person's beliefs about an existing mental condition, and that mental health locus of control scales refer to instruments that measure a person' beliefs about an existing mental condition. To our knowledge, there are no scales exclusively designed for measuring people's mental health locus of control. However, the Multidimensional Health Locus of Control (MHLC) Form C (Wallston et al., 1994) could be a helpful alternative. As Wallston et al. (1994) claim, the MHLC Form C, designed to be "condition-specific," can be used to study individuals with an existing health/medical condition by substituting whatever condition (e.g., arthritis, diabetes, pain, etc.) the subjects have for the word "condition" in each item with. As thus, we adapted it to a depression-specific instrument, as shown in Table 2.1, in which each item is a belief statement about depression with which a person may agree or disagree.

The construct above contains three subscales of depression locus of control: Internal (Items 1, 6, 8, 12, 13, and 17), Powerful Others (Items 3, 7, 5, 10, 14, and 18), and Chance (Items 2, 4, 9, 11, 15, and 16). Drawing on Wallston et al. (1994), we can propose that the Internal depression locus of control refers to the extent to which one believes his/her depression status is a function of his/her own behaviors; the Powerful Others depression locus of control refers to the belief that a person's depression status is determined by the actions of "powerful" doctors, family members, friends, etc.; and the Chance depression locus of control refers to the belief that chance, fate, or luck determines one's depression status.

The MHLC Form C can be used to measure a person's belief about where control over any of his/her specific mental conditions lies when we replace "condition" in all the items on the scale with a specific mental condition, like anxiety, personality disorder, etc. As argued by Wallston et al. (1994: 535), "in predicting behaviors or

2.2 Mental Health Locus of Control Scales

Table 2.1 Multidimensional health locus of control scale for depression

Number	Question	SD[a]	MD[b]	D[c]	A[d]	MA[e]	SA[f]
1	If my depression worsens, it is my own behavior which determines how soon I will feel better again[g]	1	2	3	4	5	6
2	As to my depression, what will be will be	1	2	3	4	5	6
3	If I see my doctor regularly, I am less likely to have problems with my depression	1	2	3	4	5	6
4	Most things that affect my depression happen to me by chance	1	2	3	4	5	6
5	Whenever my depression worsens, I should consult a medically trained professional	1	2	3	4	5	6
6	I am directly responsible for my depression getting better or worse	1	2	3	4	5	6
7	Other people play a big role in whether my depression improves, stays the same, or gets worse	1	2	3	4	5	6
8	Whatever goes wrong with my depression is my own fault	1	2	3	4	5	6
9	Luck plays a big part in determining how my depression improves	1	2	3	4	5	6
10	In order for my depression to improve, it is up to other people to see that the right things happen	1	2	3	4	5	6
11	Whatever improvement occurs with my depression is largely a matter of good fortune	1	2	3	4	5	6
12	The main thing which affects my depression is what I myself do	1	2	3	4	5	6
13	I deserve the credit when my depression improves and the blame when it gets worse	1	2	3	4	5	6
14	Following doctor's orders to the letter is the best way to keep my depression from getting any worse	1	2	3	4	5	6
15	If my depression worsens, it's a matter of fate	1	2	3	4	5	6
16	If I am lucky, my depression will get better	1	2	3	4	5	6

(continued)

Table 2.1 (continued)

Number	Question	SD[a]	MD[b]	D[c]	A[d]	MA[e]	SA[f]
17	If my depression takes a turn for the worse, it is because I have not been taking proper care of myself	1	2	3	4	5	6
18	The type of help I receive from other people determines how soon my depression improves	1	2	3	4	5	6

[a] 1 = SD (Strongly Disagree)
[b] 2 = MD (Moderately Disagree)
[c] 3 = D (Slightly Disagree)
[d] 4 = A (Slightly Agree)
[e] 5 = MA (Moderately Agree)
[f] 6 = SA (Strongly Agree)
[g] Beside each statement is a scale ranging from strongly disagree (1) to strongly agree (6). For each item we would like you to circle the number that represents the extent to which you agree or disagree with that statement. The more you agree with a statement, the higher will be the number you circle. The more you disagree with a statement, the lower will be the number you circle. Please make sure that you answer EVERY ITEM and that you circle ONLY ONE number per item. This is a measure of your personal beliefs; obviously, there are no right or wrong answers

outcomes in specific psychological situations, expectancies specific to that situation would perform better than more generalized expectancies."

We will discuss how to translate and adapt the MHLC Form C to Chinese and validate the reliability and validity of the translated and adapted Chinese measure in Chap. 3.

2.3 Attitude Assessment Scales

People living with mental disorders are far more stigmatized than individuals living with other medical conditions, leading to unfavorable individual, social, political, economic, and psychological consequences (Baumann, 2007; El-Badri & Mellsop, 2007; Marwaha & Johnson, 2005). It is, therefore, imperative to measure stigma attached to mental disorders and those living with these conditions to launch targeted stigma reduction initiatives. To this end, various instruments have been designed to capture various, mental illness-related stigma, including Day's Mental Illness Stigma Scale (Day et al., 2007), the Dementia Attitudes Scale (O'Connor & McFadden, 2010), Stigma questionnaire (Cheng et al., 2011), the Family Stigma in Alzheimer's Disease Scale (Werner et al., 2011), STIG-MA (Piver et al., 2013), Dementia Stigma Questionnaire (Woo & Chung, 2013), the Prejudice towards People with Mental Illness (PPMI) scale (Kenny et al., 2018), the Stigma-9 Questionnaire (STIG-9) (Gierka et al., 2018), the Dementia Public Stigma Scale (DPSS) (Kim et al., 2022), among many others.

2.3 Attitude Assessment Scales

Stigma, "generated in social contexts" (Goffman, 1986: 138), mainly comprises public stigma (a negative reaction to a stigmatized individual or group from non-stigmatized others), affiliated stigma (the experience of stigma in individuals associated with a stigmatized person), and self-stigma (the negative attitudes that a stigmatized person perceives from society and internalizes in himself or herself) (Corrigan & Watson, 2002). Public stigma underpins affiliated stigma and self-stigma, as found by Jones and Corrigan (2014). Based on this finding, we think it imperative to examine public stigma before studying affiliated and self-stigma. We, therefore, exemplify mental disorders-related attitude assessment tools with the Dementia Public Stigma Scale (DPSS) (Kim et al., 2022), as shown in Table 2.2.

In the DPSS, five distinct dementia-related stigma factors have been identified: "Fear and discomfort," "Incapability and loss," "Acknowledgement of personhood," "Burden," and "Exclusion." The "Fear and discomfort" factor reflects the emotional domain of stigma and discomfort around people living with dementia; the "Incapability and loss" factor reflects the cognitive domain of stigma especially lack of capability and loss of personhood; the "Acknowledgement of personhood" factor reflects

Table 2.2 The Dementia Public Stigma Scale (DPSS)

Question items	SD[a]	D	MD	Neutral	MA	A	SA
I feel confident around people with dementia	○	○	○	○	○	○	○
I am comfortable touching people with dementia	○	○	○	○	○	○	○
I feel relaxed around people with dementia	○	○	○	○	○	○	○
I am afraid of people with dementia	○	○	○	○	○	○	○
People with dementia should always be supervised	○	○	○	○	○	○	○
People with dementia are unpredictable	○	○	○	○	○	○	○
People with dementia are very much like children	○	○	○	○	○	○	○
People with dementia are incapable of making any personal decisions	○	○	○	○	○	○	○
People with dementia are no longer themselves because they have dementia	○	○	○	○	○	○	○
People with dementia can enjoy life	○	○	○	○	○	○	○
People with dementia can feel when others are kind to them	○	○	○	○	○	○	○
It is possible to enjoy interacting with people with dementia	○	○	○	○	○	○	○
People with dementia are a burden to their family	○	○	○	○	○	○	○
People with dementia are a burden on the healthcare system	○	○	○	○	○	○	○
I would exclude people with dementia from activities	○	○	○	○	○	○	○
I would ignore people with dementia	○	○	○	○	○	○	○

[a] SD = Strongly Disagree; D = Disagree; MD = Moderately Disagree; Neutral = Not disagree nor agree; MA = Moderately Agree, A = Agree; SA = Strongly Agree

the cognitive domain of stigma and understanding of people living with dementia; the "Burden" factor reflects the cognitive domain of stigma and perceptions that people living with dementia are a burden to family and society; and the "Exclusion" factor reflects the behavioral domain of stigma and the display of discriminatory behaviors (Kim et al., 2022).

We will discuss how to translate and adapt the DPSS to Chinese and validate the reliability and validity of the translated and adapted Chinese instrument in Chap. 4.

2.4 Summary

In this chapter, we present two main categories of mental health scales: (1) mental health locus of control scales and (2) attitude assessment tools. The mental health locus of control scales measures a person' beliefs about an existing mental condition, like the Multidimensional Depression Locus of Control Scale Form C. The attitude assessment tools are designed to measure people's attitudes towards mental disorders, as illustrated by the Dementia Public Stigma Scale (DPSS). The translation and adaptation of these two types of scales will be discussed in Chaps. 3 and 4 respectively.

References

Baumann, A. (2007). Stigmatization, social distance and exclusion because of mental illness: The individual with mental illness as a 'stranger.' *International Review of Psychiatry, 19*(2), 131–135.

Blais, M., & Baer, L. (2010). Understanding rating scales and assessment instruments. In L. Baer & M. A. Blais (Eds.), *Handbook of clinical rating scales and assessment in psychiatry and mental health* (pp. 1–6). Humana Press.

Cheng, S., Lam, L. C. W., Chan, L. C. K., et al. (2011). The effects of exposure to scenarios about dementia on stigma and attitudes toward dementia care in a Chinese community. *International Psychogeriatrics, 23*(9), 1433–1441.

Compton, M. T., Hankerson-Dyson, D., & Broussard, B. (2011). Development, item analysis, and initial reliability and validity of a multiple-choice knowledge of mental illnesses test for lay samples. *Psychiatry Research, 189*, 141–148.

Corrigan, P. W., & Watson, A. C. (2002). Understanding the impact of stigma on people with mental illness. *World Psychiatry, 1*(1), 16–20.

Crisp, A., Gelder, M. G., Goddard, E., & Meltzer, H. (2005). Stigmatization of people with mental illnesses: A follow-up study within the changing minds campaign of the royal college of psychiatrists. *World Psychiatry, 4*, 106–113.

Day, E. N., Edgren, K., & Eshleman, A. (2007). Measuring stigma toward mental illness: Development and application of the mental illness stigma scale. *Journal of Applied Social Psychology, 37*(10), 2191–2219.

Demyttenaere, K., Bruffaerts, R., Posada-Villa, J., Gasquet, I., et al. (2004). Prevalence, severity, and unmet need for treatment of mental disorders in the world health organization world mental health surveys. *JAMA, 292*(21), 2581–2590.

Dunn, K. I., Goldney, R. D., DalGrande, E., & Taylor, A. (2009). Quantification and examination of depression-related mental health literacy. *Journal of Evaluation in Clinical Practice, 15*, 650–653.

References

El-Badri, S., & Mellsop, G. (2007). Stigma and quality of life as experienced by people with mental illness. *Australasian Psychiatry, 15*, 195–200.

Gierka, B., Löwea, B., Murraya, A. M., & Kohlmann, S. (2018). Assessment of perceived mental health-related stigma: The Stigma-9 Questionnaire (STIG-9). *Psychiatry Research, 270*, 822–830.

Goffman, E. (1986). *Stigma: Notes on the management of spoiled identity.* Simon & Schuster (Original work published 1963).

Jones, N., & Corrigan, P. W. (2014). Understanding stigma. In P. W. Corrigan (Ed.), *The stigma of disease and disability: Understanding causes and overcoming injustices* (pp. 9–34). American Psychological Association.

Jorm, A. F., Korten, A. E., Jacomb, P. A., Christensen, H., Rodgers, B., & Pollitt, P. (1997). 'Mental health literacy': A survey of the public's ability to recognize mental disorders and their beliefs about the effectiveness of treatment. *Medical Journal of Australia, 166*, 182–186.

Jorm, A. F., Barney, L. J., Christensen, H., Highet, N. J., Kelly, C. M., & Kitchener, B. A. (2006). Research on mental health literacy: What we know and what we still need to know. *Australian and New Zealand Journal of Psychiatry, 40*, 3–5.

Kenny, A., Bizumic, B., & Griffiths, K. M. (2018). The Prejudice towards People with Mental Illness (PPMI) scale: Structure and validity. *BMC Psychiatry, 18*, 293.

Kim, S., Eccleston, C., Klekociuk, S., Cook, P. S., & Doherty, K. (2022). Development and psychometric evaluation of the dementia public stigma scale. *International Journal of Geriatric Psychiatry, 37*(2), 1–9.

Lauber, C., Nordt, C., Falcato, L., & Rossler, W. (2003). Do people recognize mental illness? Factors influencing mental health literacy. *European Archives of Psychiatry and Clinical Neuroscience, 253*, 248–251.

Marwaha, S., & Johnson, S. (2005). Views and experiences of employment among people with psychosis: A qualitative descriptive study. *International Journal of Social Psychiatry, 51*, 302–316.

Mental Health Foundation. (2016). *Fundamental facts about mental health 2016.* Mental Health Foundation.

O'Connor, M. L., & McFadden, S. H. (2010). Development and psychometric validation of the dementia attitudes scales. *International Journal of Alzheimer's Disease, 4*, 1–10.

O'Connor, M., & Casey, L. (2015). The Mental Health Literacy Scale (MHLS): A new scale-based measure of mental health literacy. *Psychiatry Research, 229*, 511–516.

Piver, L. C., Nubukpo, P., Faure, A., Dumoitier, N., Couratier, P., & Clément, J. P. (2013). Describing perceived stigma against Alzheimer's disease in a general population in France: The STIGMA survey. *International Journal of Geriatric Psychiatry, 28*(9), 933–938.

Rush, A. J., Trivedi, M. H., Ibrahim, H. M., et al. (2003). The 16-item Quick Inventory of Depressive Symptomatology (QIDS), Clinician Rating (QIDS-C), and Self-Report (QIDS-SR): A psychometric evaluation in patients with chronic major depression. *Biological Psychiatry, 54*, 573–583.

UN News: Global perspective Human stories. (2022). *Nearly one billion people have a mental disorder.* WHO. https://news.un.org/en/story/2022/06/1120682

Vos, T., Barber, R. M., Bell, B., Bertozzi-Villa, A., Biryukov, S., Bolliger, I., et al. (2013). Global, regional, and national incidence, prevalence, and years lived with disability for 301 acute and chronic diseases and injuries in 188 countries, 1990–2013: A systematic analysis for the global burden of disease study. *The Lancet, 386*(9995), 743–800.

Wallston, K. A., Stein, M. J., & Smith, C. A. (1994). Form C of MHLC scales: A condition-specific measure of locus of control. *Journal of Personality Assessment, 63*, 534–553.

Wallston, K. A. (2023). *Multidimensional Health Locus of Control (MHLC) scales.* https://nursing.vanderbilt.edu/projects/wallstonk/index.php. Accessed July 8, 2023.

Werner, P., Goldstein, D., & Heinik, J. (2011). Development and validity of the Family Stigma in Alzheimer's Disease Scale (FS–ADS). *Alzheimer Disease Associated Disorders, 25*(1), 42–48.

Woo, B. K. P., & Chung, J. O. P. (2013). Public stigma associated with dementia in a Chinese-American immigrant population. *Journal of the American Geriatrics Society, 61*(10), 1832–1833.

Open Access This chapter is licensed under the terms of the Creative Commons Attribution-NonCommercial-NoDerivatives 4.0 International License (http://creativecommons.org/licenses/by-nc-nd/4.0/), which permits any noncommercial use, sharing, distribution and reproduction in any medium or format, as long as you give appropriate credit to the original author(s) and the source, provide a link to the Creative Commons license and indicate if you modified the licensed material. You do not have permission under this license to share adapted material derived from this chapter or parts of it.

The images or other third party material in this chapter are included in the chapter's Creative Commons license, unless indicated otherwise in a credit line to the material. If material is not included in the chapter's Creative Commons license and your intended use is not permitted by statutory regulation or exceeds the permitted use, you will need to obtain permission directly from the copyright holder.

Chapter 3
Translating and Adapting the Multidimensional Health Locus of Control Scale FORM C to a Chinese Scale Specifically Used for Measuring People's Beliefs About the Prevention and Treatment of Depression in Mainland China

Abstract Depression is a common mental disorder that besets an estimated 5% of adults worldwide. The health locus of control construct is likely to mediate health status and outcomes, and it has proven helpful in predicting and explaining specific health-related behaviors. However, it has never been used to investigate health beliefs about the prevention and treatment of depression. This chapter translates and adapts the MHLC Form C to Chinese and makes the Chinese version depression specific.

Keywords Health beliefs · Multidimensional Health Locus of Control · Translation and adaptation · Prevention and treatment · Depression · Chinese patients · Latent class analysis · Low efficacy · Contributing factors

3.1 Background

Depressive disorder (also known as depression) is a common mental disorder that involves a depressed mood or loss of pleasure or interest in activities for long periods of time (World Health Organization, 2023). Different from regular mood changes and feelings about everyday life, depression can impact all aspects of life, such as relationships with family, friends and community (World Health Organization, 2023). It can stem from or result in problems at school or at work.

Depression may afflict anyone, especially those who have experienced abuse, severe losses or other stressful events (World Health Organization, 2023). It is estimated that about 3.8% of the population worldwide suffer from depressive disorder, including around 5% of adults (4% of men and 6% of women), and 5.7% of older adults aged over 60 years (World Health Organization, 2023). About 280 million people worldwide have depression (Institute of Health Metrics and Evaluation, 2023).

Women are more likely to develop depression than men: depression is estimated to be about 50% more common among women than among men (World Health Organization, 2023). Over 10% of pregnant women and postpartum women suffer from depression (Woody et al., 2017). Depression can lead to suicide, which claims the life of more than 700,000 people annually and ranks the fourth leading cause of death among those who are aged between 15 and 29 years (World Health Organization, 2023).

Regardless of known, effective treatments of mental illnesses, over 75% of people in low- and middle-income countries are untreated (Evans-Lacko et al., 2018) due to various obstacles to effective care, including a lack of investment in mental health care, a lack of trained healthcare providers and social stigma attached to mental disorders (World Health Organization, 2023).

Depressive disorder stems from the complex interplay between social, physical, psychological, and biological factors (World Health Organization, 2023). Individuals who have experienced adverse life events (e.g., unemployment, bereavement, traumatic events, etc.) are more likely to develop depression, which can, in turn, result in more stress and dysfunction and worsen the affected person's life situation (World Health Organization, 2023). Many factors that influence depression (e.g., physical inactivity, abuse of alcohol, etc.) are known risk factors for diseases including cardiovascular disease, cancer, diabetes and respiratory diseases, which, in turn, make people experience depression because of the difficulties in managing their condition (World Health Organization, 2023).

Depression can be effectively treated. Effective treatments include psychological treatment and antidepressant medications. Psychological treatments include teaching new ways of thinking, coping with or relating to others, talk therapy with professionals and supervised lay therapists, behavioral activation, cognitive behavioral therapy, interpersonal psychotherapy, and problem-solving therapy (World Health Organization, 2023).

Depression can be effectively reduced through some prevention programs. These programs include school-based programs to enhance a pattern of positive coping in children and adolescents, interventions for parents of children with behavioral problems, exercise programs for older persons, and self-care (World Health Organization, 2023). Self-care can effectively facilitate managing depression symptoms and promoting overall well-being (World Health Organization, 2023). It takes on many different forms, including trying to keep doing activities one used to enjoy, exercising regularly, sticking to regular eating and sleeping habits as much as possible, avoiding or cutting down on alcohol and not using illicit drugs, staying connected with friends and family, talking to someone one trusts about one's feelings, seeking help from a healthcare provider, joining a support group, etc. (World Health Organization, 2023).

WHO's Mental Health Action Plan 2013–2030 emphasizes the essential steps to provide appropriate interventions for individuals with mental illnesses including depression. Two categories of interventions are highlighted: increasing services for people with mental, neurological and substance use disorders through care provided by health workers, and developing psychological, group-treatment, and cognitive-behavioral intervention manuals (World Health Organization, 2023).

3.1 Background

The treatments, prevention programs and interventions above can fall into three types of locus of control: the affected person's internal motivation, health and medical professionals and other people (e.g., family, friends, those one trusts, etc.). These three types of health locus of control have already been captured in previous studies (Donovan & O'Leary, 1978; Gebhardt et al., 2001; Lewis et al., 1978; Macleod & Macleod, 1998; Martin, 1999; Martin & Jomeen, 2004; Martin et al., 1990; Pastor et al., 1993; Saltzer, 1982; Strudler-Wallston & Wallston, 1978; Wallston et al., 1976). However, the treatments, prevention programs and interventions proposed by World Health Organization (2023) have not involved the affected people's belief about the influence of chance on the prevention and treatment of depression, which has been proven important for health-related behaviors and health outcomes by Wallston et al (1994). Informed by these studies, we hypothesized that the prevention and treatment of depression could be impacted by four different types of health locus of control measured by the four subscales of the Multidimensional Health Locus of Control Scale (MHLC) Form C, 'internal,' 'chance,' 'powerful other people,' and 'doctors,' respectively, which should be investigated to deliver tailor-made education and interventions. Based on this hypothesis, we raised our research questions: how many clusters can the study participants be grouped into based on their attitudes towards and beliefs about the prevention and treatment of depression, specifically their beliefs about the source of reinforcements for health-related behaviors if they develop depression? Can such beliefs be associated with the participants' demographic features and health literacy status?

Patients' attitudes towards the conditions from which they are suffering can be measured by the locus of control (LOC) construct, as extensively demonstrated by a huge variety of pathology (Donovan & O'Leary, 1978; Lewis et al., 1978; Saltzer, 1982; Martin et al., 1990; Macleod & Macleod, 1998; Pastor et al., 1993). It had been clinically observed that the LOC construct can mediate health status and outcomes (Gebhardt et al., 2001; Martin, 1999; Martin & Jomeen, 2004; Strudler-Wallston & Wallston, 1978; Wallston et al., 1976), and it has proven helpful in predicting and explaining specific health-related behaviors (Strudler-Wallston & Wallston, 1978). Based on the LOC construct, individuals can be categorized into two main classes: those believing that their health status (or sickness) results from their own behaviors ('health-internals') and those considering that their health status is generally determined by factors over which they have poor control, like chance or powerful others ('health-externals') (Wallston et al., 1976). Wallston et al. later proved the importance of assessing beliefs in the influence of chance and powerful others separately (Wallston et al., 1978). More recently, Wallston et al. (1994) have shown that it is also helpful to distinguish between expectations related to doctors and those related to significant others (e.g., relatives, friends, etc.) within the 'powerful others' construct. Health LOC has been conceptualized as a construct comprising at least 3 dimensions (Wallston et al., 1978). The most extensively used, validated instrument of LOC in health is the Multidimensional Health Locus of Control Scale (MHLC) (Wallston et al., 1978). This measure consists of 18 items that are rated on a 6-point Likert scale ranging from strongly disagree ($= 1$) to strongly agree ($= 6$). These 18 items are divided into 3 6-item subscales that measure 'internal,' 'chance,' and 'powerful others' LOC. Higher scores for each subscale indicate greater belief in that subscale domain in relation to health. There are 3 refined versions of the MHLC, namely, the MHLC Form A, the MHLC Form B, and the MHLC Form C (Wallston et al., 1994). The MHLC Form C consists of 4 subscales, 'internal' (6 items), 'chance' (6 items), 'powerful other people' (3 items), and 'doctors' (3 items) (Wallston et al., 1978).

The MHLC Form C has been applied to enhance the knowledge about the HIV + patients' point of view of their complex health condition (Ubbiali et al., 2008), determine how LOC relates to health care use, medication adherence, missed school, and readiness for transition to adult medical care for youths with chronic conditions (Nazareth et al., 2016), explore the relationship between LOC and pregnancy (Green et al., 1990; Lavender et al., 1999; Pang et al., 2001; Scott-Palmer & Skevington, 1981; Tinsley et al., 1993), etc. However, it has never been translated and adapted to Chinese and used exclusively for measuring people's beliefs about the prevention and treatment of depression in mainland China. In the context that there is no such a scale that has been designed in Chinese for this particular purpose, it is necessary to translate and adapt the MHLC Form C to Chinese for research. Considering that the MHLC Form C is a "general purposes condition-specific locus of control scale that could easily be adapted for use with any medical or health-related condition" (Wallston et al., 1994), we adapted it for use with depression in the questionnaire we designed for our study. We believe that this adapted scale is most likely to solicit patients' attitudes towards the prevention and treatment of depression, based on which tailor-made education, intervention and treatment could be delivered for the benefit of the prevention and treatment of this disease. However, it has never been used in this respect. Considering the magnitude of depression among people in China, it is imperative to examine patients' attitudes towards and beliefs about the prevention and treatment of this disease to deliver more targeted education, intervention, prevention and treatment so as to reduce its prevalence and the mortality rate caused by it.

The objective of this study was threefold. First, we aimed to translate and adapt the MHLC Form C to Chinese and make the Chinese version depression specific. And then, we used the depression-specific Chinese version to classify the patient participants into different latent classes according to their attitudes towards and beliefs about the prevention and treatment of depression, and identified significant factors that were closely associated with the low-efficacy cluster to provide essential implications for the delivery of tailored education and interventions and the administering of targeted prevention and treatment.

3.2 Methods

3.2.1 *Translation and Adaptation of the MHLC Form C*

The symmetrical translation approach was adopted to ensure more accurate adaptation and cross-cultural validation of the Chinese version of the MHLC Form C. This approach is the most recommended methodology due to the top priority it gives to faithfulness of meaning and colloquial expressions in both the source and target languages rather than to word-for-word literal translation (Jones & Kay, 1992). It is the only method that facilitates the comparison of responses provided by individuals from one culture with those given by people from another culture (Jones & Kay, 1992; Jones et al., 2001) and the establishment of the most relevant types of cross-cultural equivalence (semantic, conceptual, content, technical and criterion) (Hilton & Skrutkowski, 2002). Although back-translation was the most commonly used methodology in the translation of mental health materials (Barger et al., 2010), back-translation cannot really ensure equivalence, particularly when many terms associated with mental health are extremely challenging or even impossible to translate directly (Barger et al., 2010). As a result, we used the "decentering" strategy rather than backward translation to increase the likelihood of translation success (Brislin et al., 1973). Decentering enables translators to consider the target and source texts equal in importance by allowing modification of the source text during the process of translation (Brislin et al., 1973). It is designed to facilitate establishing equivalence between the source and target texts. In the decentering process, we not only allowed both the source and target languages to shape decision-making in translation but also allowed the target language and culture to influence the source text (Black, 2018). In the whole translation process, we adhered to the "centering" (Brislin, 1970) principle, which attaches equal importance to both the source (English) language and the target (Chinese) language.

In this chapter, we will go through the steps of the cross-cultural validation of depression scales. These steps, as shown below, "incorporated the most recommended ones in a user-friendly guideline to facilitate adoption, consistency and use" (Sousa & Rojjanasrirat, 2011: 269).

3.2.1.1 Forward Translation of the MHLC Form C into Chinese

The MHLC Form C in the source English language was forward translated to the target Chinese language by two independent translators (Meng Ji and Yi Shan), whose mother language is the desired target Chinese language. These translators are bilingual (i.e., fluent in English and Chinese) and bi-cultural (i.e., having in-depth experience in Chinese and English culture. Both translators are trained in the use of "health care terminology and the content area of the construct" (Sousa & Rojjanasrirat, 2011: 269) of the MHLC Form C in Chinese, and the use of "colloquial phrases, health care slang and jargon, idiomatic expressions, and emotional terms in common use" (Sousa & Rojjanasrirat, 2011: 269). We developed two translated versions using words and sentences that cover both the medical and the usual spoken (colloquial) language with its cultural nuances. After that, we discussed the two versions with three medical professionals (Zhaogang Dong, Zhaoquan Xing, and Xiaofei Xu from Qilu Hospital of Shandong University, China) to minimize inconsistencies potentially introduced by the two independent translators.

3.2.1.2 Comparison of the Two Translated Chinese Versions of the MHLC Form C

A third bilingual and bi-cultural translator (Weiwei Chu) compared not only the instructions, items and responses of the two forward-translated Chinese versions but also the two Chinese versions with the original English version of the MHLC From C to identify "ambiguities and discrepancies of words, sentences and meanings" (Sousa & Rojjanasrirat, 2011: 269). Any potential ambiguities and discrepancies were discussed and resolved through discussions among the research team (Meng Ji, Yi Shan, Weiwei Chu, Zhaogang Dong, Zhaoquan Xing, and Xiaofei Xu). When consensus was reached among all members of the research team, the preliminary initial translated Chinese version of the MHLC From C was generated.

3.2.1.3 Pilot Testing of the Preliminary Initial Translated Chinese Version of the MHLC from C with a Chinese Sample: Cognitive Debriefing

The preliminary initial translated Chinese version of the MHLC From C was pilot tested among native Chinese patient participants to evaluate the instructions, items, responses of the translated instrument for clarity. Since a sample size of 10–40 informants is recommended in previous studies (Beaton et al., 2000; Sousa et al., 2009), we recruited ten volunteers for a cognitive interview, including five women and five men with year 6, year 9, year 12, and university education who were aged 32 to 66 years old. Based on the "think-aloud protocol" (Jääskeliänien, 2010), they were asked to provide open feedback on whether and how they understood the questionnaire while "thinking aloud" (Zeugfang, 2018). This step aimed to test the comprehensibility of the preliminary initial translated Chinese version of the MHLC From C. Subsequently, the 10 volunteers and all researchers of this study (Meng Ji, Yi Shan, Weiwei Chu, Zhaogang Dong, Zhaoquan Xing, and Xiaofei Xu) resolved problems with the question organization, the instrument layout (including the font size), and elusive questions or concepts (Barros et al., 2022). We focused on challenging questions and concepts related primarily to cultural relevance (whether they were relevant to the participants' daily life) and linguistic accessibility (whether they were comprehensible or ambiguous to the participants) (Shan & Ji, 2023). This step ensured the face validity (Shan & Ji, 2023) and the conceptual, semantic and content equivalence (Sousa & Rojjanasrirat, 2011), and further allowed the structure of sentences used in

3.2 Methods 23

the translated Chinese tool to be easily understood by the target patient population before psychometric testing (Sousa & Rojjanasrirat, 2011).

3.2.2 Using the Chinese MHLC Form C to Classify Patients and Identifying Factors Associated with Low Self-efficacy

3.2.2.1 Questionnaire Design

We designed a five-section questionnaire, including (1) Section 1: age, gender, education, and self-reported disease knowledge, (2) Section 2: the Chinese version of the All Aspects of Health Literacy Scale (AAHLS) (https://healthliteracy.bu.edu/documents/34/AAHLS%20Tool.pdf; Chinn & McCarthy, 2013), (3) Section 3: the Chinese version of the eHealth Literacy Scale (eHEALS) (Koo et al., 2012), (4) Section 4: the Chinese version of the General Health Numeracy Test (GHNT-6) (https://healthliteracy.bu.edu/documents/36/GHNT_6%20.pdf; Shan et al., 2023a, 2023b), and (5) Section 5: the translated and adapted Chinese version of the Multidimensional Health Locus of Control Scale (MHLC) Form C (Wallston et al., 1994). Literacy in health information is becoming a critical factor that is essential for health status (Berkman et al., 2011). The ASHLS consists of three sub-scales, functional, communicative, and critical, which play different roles (Chinn & McCarthy, 2013; Nutbeam, 2000; Shan et al., 2023a, 2023b). The functional health literacy (FHL) sub-scale contains 3 related questions regarding one's ability to comprehend health information (FHL1), seek help (FHL2), and complete formal documents (FHL3) (Nutbeam, 2000). The sum of the FHL sub-scale increases with one's functional health literacy, as higher FHL sum scores are indicative of greater capability to independently comprehend health materials, complete official documents, and effectively obtain help from others (Shan et al., 2023a, 2023b). Communicative health literacy (COHL) comprises two components: information gathering and processing skills, and interactive skills essential for successful consultations with health providers (Chinn & McCarthy, 2013; Nutbeam, 2000). Higher COHL sum scores are indicative of lower COHL (Shan et al., 2023a, 2023b). The critical health literacy (CRHL) sub-scale of the AAHLS assesses one's ability to evaluate the quality of health materials consciously, critically, purposefully from various sources including internet, one's engagement with health professionals, and acting at both individual and community levels. Chinn and McCarthy (Chinn & McCarthy, 2013) investigated the relationship between the total AAHLS score and the sub-scale scores with sex, ethnicity, and reported presence of a long-term health condition. The 8-item eHEALS evaluates the study participants' knowledge and skills that are essential for using eHealth resources and interventions (Koo et al., 2012).

The GHNT has 6 related questions about one's ability to comprehend and utilize simple quantitative health materials. As a result, a higher sum score of the GHNT indicates lower general health numeracy skills (Shan et al., 2023a, 2023b). The 18-item MHLC Form C comprises 4 subscales that measure 'Internal,' 'Chance,' 'Doctor,' and 'Powerful Others' locus of control, that is, beliefs that the source of reinforcements for health-related behaviors is primarily internal, a matter of chance, or under the control of doctors or powerful others (Wallston et al., 1994). Such beliefs can motivate health behavior, which refers to taking voluntary actions to promote health, reduce health risks (Sarafino, 2006), and mediate health status (Jomeen & Martin, 2002). Individuals categorized as having an 'Internal' locus of control are more likely to engage in health behaviors and are more knowledgeable regarding their health problems (Bane et al., 2006; Takaki and Yano 2006). Considering that the MHLC Form C is a "general purposes condition-specific locus of control scale that could easily be adapted for use with any medical or health-related condition" (Wallston et al., 1994), we adapted it for use with depression in the questionnaire. Informed by relevant studies (Martin, 1999; Berkman et al., 2011; Sarafino, 2006; Jomeen & Martin, 2002; Bane et al., 2006; Takaki & Yano, 2006), we hypothesized that the participants' status of health belief and self-confidence measured by the MHLC Form C in Section 5 could be closely associated with information collected through Sections 1–4.

3.2.2.2 Participant Recruitment and Questionnaire Survey

The study participants were recruited from Qilu Hospital of Shandong University, China, using randomized sampling. Participants who had met four predefined inclusion criteria were invited to participate in this survey: (1) being aged ≥ 18 years, (2) having at least primary education (Year 6 schooling) to understand the questions in the questionnaire, (3) being patients rather than relatives accompanying patients, and (4) participating in the survey voluntarily. We made face-to-face contact with Mandarin Chinese-speaking patients who were attending the outpatient clinic and those who were hospitalized to identify those who satisfied the inclusion criteria, explain to them about the purpose of the survey, and ask them to participate in the web-based survey as scheduled. We identified 1208 eligible patients.

The survey lasted one month from July 20, 2022, to August 19, 2022. The questionnaire was administered via *wenjuanxing* (https://www.wjx.cn/ [accessed 2022-07-21]), the most popular web-based questionnaire platform in China. Participants filled out the administered questionnaire on the web. Returned questionnaires were considered valid only when all question items included were answered according to our predefined validation criterion. On August 20, 2022, the returned questionnaires were downloaded in the format of an Excel file (Microsoft Corp) from *wenjuanxing*. A total of 988 answered questionnaires were returned, with a response rate of 81.8% (988/1208). We double-checked the returned questionnaires and found all of them to be valid.

3.2 Methods

3.2.2.3 Data Collection, Coding and Analysis

On August 20, 2022, the answered questionnaires were downloaded in the format of an EXCEL file from *wenjuanxing*. We double checked the validity of the returned questionnaires before coding valid data using the predefined coding schemes based on Likert scales with varying score ranges for different questionnaire items. After that, we used latent class modelling (LCA; Latent GOLD 5.0) to classify the patient participants into different clusters according to the their status of health attitudes and belief measured by the translated Chinese version of the MHLC Form C which had been made depression-specific, and identified factors significantly associated with the low-efficacy cluster.

LCA is increasingly applied in social and health sciences. LCA has methodological advantages over traditional clustering techniques (Nylund-Gibso & Choi, 2018; Tein, 2013; Morovati, 2014; Morgan, 2014). A notable benefit of LCA is the probabilistic attribution of latent class membership to study participants using maximum likelihood estimation (Nylund-Gibso & Choi, 2018). As a result, each observed participant attains a probability of belonging to a certain latent class. For example, within a 2-class LCA solution, a study participant can have 2 probabilities associated with either latent class. The combined probabilities of class memberships sum to 1, based on the conditional independence assumption of LCA. The probabilistic nature of LCA adds to the complexity of the result interpretation. However, in practice, the more flexible, intuitive approach of LCA when compared with "hard, rigid" clustering techniques allows researchers more insights into the impact of predictor variables on latent class membership fluidity and dynamics, as well as the susceptibility of class memberships to the definition and selection of probability thresholds to suit different research purposes.

3.2.2.4 Ethics Approval

This study was approved by the Ethics Review Board of Qilu Hospital of Shandong University, China. The review number is KYLL-202208-026. The study data were anonymized to protect the privacy and confidentiality of the study participants. Because the participants voluntarily participated in the survey to support and promote academic research, no compensation was provided for them as per the common practice in China.

3.3 Results

3.3.1 Translation and Adaptation of the MHLC Form C

3.3.1.1 Forward Translation of the MHLC Form C into Chinese

Two translated versions were produced independently by two translators using words and sentences that cover both medical and usual spoken (colloquial) language with its cultural nuances. Table 3.1 was translated by Yi Shan, and Table 3.2 was translated by Meng Ji.

When discussing these two versions with Zhaogang Dong, Zhaoquan Xing, and Xiaofei Xu from Qilu Hospital of Shandong University, we did not identify idiosyncrasies that had been introduced by the two independent translators. These two versions were then subjected to further analysis in Sects. 4.3.1.2 and 4.3.1.3.

3.3.1.2 Comparison of the Two Translated Chinese Versions of the MHLC Form C

The third bilingual and bi-cultural translator (Weiwei Chu) compared the two translated Chinese versions and checked these two Chinese versions against the original English version. It was found that although these two versions were largely semantically equivalent to the original English version, some discrepancies of words and sentences between the two Chinese versions were identified in terms of Items 3, 10, 11, 13, 15, and 18, as has been marked with bold font in Tables 3.1 and 3.2. To make comparison convenient, these items from both tables are presented in Table 3.3.

As can be seen from Table 3.3, Versions 1 and 2 showed different degrees of adaptation in which the wording and sentence structures have been adjusted to produce colloquial and idiomatic translated items that are more likely to be culturally relevant, comprehensible, and acceptable to Chinese readers. Some problems were found in these two translated versions. As the third translator pointed out, the wording and sentence structures of some translated items needed to be modified to make them more linguistically and culturally appropriate or adapted although the translated versions were largely understandable. In other words, the translated versions needed to be revised in terms of colloquial and idiomatic expressions that were more culturally relevant, understandable, and acceptable by means of various translation techniques including addition and deletion, literal and liberal translation, recasting, and so on. To this end, the research team (Meng Ji, Yi Shan, Weiwei Chu, Zhaogang Dong, Zhaoquan Xing, and Xiaofei Xu) discussed any potential ambiguities and discrepancies round after round until consensuses were reached among all team members. The results of discussion are presented item after item in the following paragraphs.

First, "see my doctor" in Item 3 was translated into "去找医生治疗" ("visit a doctor for treatment") and "看医生" ("see a doctor") in Version 1 and Version 2 respectively, but these two Chinese translations were changed to "看病" ("treat my

3.3 Results

Table 3.1 Chinese Version 1 of the MHLC Form C

编号	观念	非常不赞同	基本不赞同	有点不赞同	有点赞同	基本赞同	非常赞同
1	如果我的抑郁症恶化,我自己的行为决定了我多久会再次好转。	1	2	3	4	5	6
2	我的抑郁症好转还是加重就顺其自然吧。	1	2	3	4	5	6
3	如果我定期去找医生治疗,我的抑郁症就不太可能出现问题。	1	2	3	4	5	6
4	大多数影响我抑郁症的因素都是偶然发生在我身上的。	1	2	3	4	5	6
5	每当我的抑郁症恶化时,我应该咨询受过医学培训的专业人士。	1	2	3	4	5	6
6	我的抑郁症好转还是恶化直接取决于我自己。	1	2	3	4	5	6
7	我的抑郁症是否好转、保持不变或者恶化,其他人起很大作用。	1	2	3	4	5	6
8	无论我的抑郁症出现什么样的恶化,都是我自己的问题。	1	2	3	4	5	6
9	我的抑郁症改善情况在很大程度上是由运气决定的。	1	2	3	4	5	6
10	为了改善我的抑郁症,其他人必须确保不出差错。	1	2	3	4	5	6
11	无论我的抑郁症出现什么程度的改善,很大程度上都纯属幸运。	1	2	3	4	5	6
12	影响我抑郁的主要因素是我自己的所作所为。	1	2	3	4	5	6
13	我的抑郁症好转归功于我自己,我的抑郁症恶化也怪我自己。	1	2	3	4	5	6
14	遵从医嘱是防止我的抑郁症恶化的最好方法。	1	2	3	4	5	6
15	如果我的抑郁症恶化,那就是命运的问题了。	1	2	3	4	5	6
16	如果我幸运的话,我的抑郁症会好转起来。	1	2	3	4	5	6
17	如果我的抑郁症恶化,那是因为我没有好好照顾自己。	1	2	3	4	5	6
18	我从其他人那里得到什么样的帮助决定了我的抑郁症好转的快慢。	1	2	3	4	5	6

Table 3.2 Chinese Version 2 of the MHLC Form C

编号	观念	非常不赞同	基本不赞同	有点不赞同	有点赞同	基本赞同	非常赞同
1	如果我的抑郁症病情恶化,我自己的行为决定了我多久会再次好转。	1	2	3	4	5	6
2	我的抑郁症病情就顺其自然吧。	1	2	3	4	5	6
3	如果我定期看医生,我的抑郁症症状就会少出些问题。	1	2	3	4	5	6
4	大多数影响我抑郁症病情的因素都是偶然发生在我身上的。	1	2	3	4	5	6
5	每当我的抑郁症病情恶化时,我应该咨询受过医学培训的专业人士。	1	2	3	4	5	6
6	我的抑郁症病情好转还是恶化直接取决于我自己。	1	2	3	4	5	6
7	我的抑郁症病情是否好转、保持不变或者恶化,其他人起很大作用。	1	2	3	4	5	6
8	无论我的抑郁症病情出现什么样的恶化,都是我自己的问题。	1	2	3	4	5	6
9	我的抑郁症病情改善情况在很大程度上是由运气决定的。	1	2	3	4	5	6
10	为了改善我的抑郁症病情,其他人要确保不犯错误。	1	2	3	4	5	6
11	如果我的抑郁症多多少少有了好转,那都是我走运。	1	2	3	4	5	6
12	影响我抑郁症病情的主要因素是我自己的所作所为。	1	2	3	4	5	6
13	我的抑郁症变好变坏都在我自己。	1	2	3	4	5	6
14	遵从医嘱是防止我的抑郁症病情恶化的最好方法。	1	2	3	4	5	6
15	如果我的抑郁症恶化,那是我的命。	1	2	3	4	5	6
16	如果我幸运的话,我的抑郁症病情会好转起来。	1	2	3	4	5	6
17	如果我的抑郁症病情恶化,那是因为我没有好好照顾自己。	1	2	3	4	5	6
18	别人给我的照顾多一些,我的抑郁症就好得快一些;别人给我的照顾少一些,我的抑郁症就好得慢一些。	1	2	3	4	5	6

Table 3.3 Comparison of translated Versions 1 and 2 with the original English version of the MHLC Form C

编号	Original English Version	Translated Version 1	Translated Version 2
3	If I **see my doctor**[a] regularly, I **am less likely to have problems with** my depression	如果我定期去找医生治疗[a],我的抑郁症病情就不太可能出现问题。	如果我定期看医生[a],我的抑郁症症状就会少出些问题。
10	In order for my depression to improve, it **is up to** other people to **see that the right things happen**	为了改善我的抑郁症病情,其他人必须确保不出差错。	为了改善我的抑郁症病情,其他人要确保不犯错误。
11	**Whatever improvement** occurs with my depression **is largely a matter of good fortune**	无论我的抑郁症出现什么程度的改善,很大程度上都纯属幸运。	如果我的抑郁症多多少少有了好转,那都是我走运。
13	**I deserve the credit when** my depression **improves** and **the blame when** it **gets worse**	我的抑郁症病情好转归功于我自己,我的抑郁症病情恶化也怪我自己。	我的抑郁症变好变坏都在我自己。
15	If my **depression** worsens, **it's a matter of fate**	如果我的抑郁症病情恶化,那就是命运的问题了。	如果我的抑郁症恶化,那是我的命。
18	**The type of help I receive from other people determines how soon my depression improves**	我从其他人那里得到什么样的帮助决定了我的抑郁症病情好转的快慢。	别人给我的照顾多一些,我的抑郁症就好得快一些;别人给我的照顾少一些,我的抑郁症就好得慢一些。

[a] The bold font in the six items under the column headers of "Original English Version," "Translated Version 1," and "Translated Version 2" indicates where there are discrepancies between the two Chinese versions in terms of wording and sentence structures

disease") which was considered as more habitually used by and more culturally relevant to Chinese populations in their daily life. By contrast, "看医生" ("see a doctor"), though understandable to Chinese people, is less culturally relevant and acceptable in the Chinese context, due to the fact that people usually do not have their private doctor but go to hospital to visit a doctor for treatment if they are ill. "去找医生治疗" ("visit a doctor for treatment"), although understandable, is less colloquial and idiomatic compared with "看病" ("treat my disease") which is the most used expression among Chinese people. The Chinese translations of "am less likely to have problems with" in Item 3, "病情就不太可能出现问题" ("problems are less likely to occur to my condition") in Version 1 and "症状就会少出些问题" ("less problems are likely to occur to my symptoms") in Version 2, were changed to "就不大会出问题" ("am less likely to have problems") for more colloquial and idiomatic expression and thus for greater acceptability to Chinese readers based on their lived experiences.

In the translation of Item 10, "is up to" and "to see" was combined into "必须确保" ("must ensure") in Version 1 and "要确保" ("need to ensure") in Version 2, and "that the right things happen" was translated and adapted to "不出差错" ("there are no slips") in Version 1 and "不犯错误" ("no mistakes are made") in Version 2. After discussion, we decided to change these adapted translations to "做该做的事情" As a result, the whole item, "In order for my depression to improve, it is up to other people to see that the right things happen." was revised to "要让我的抑郁症好转，其他人要为我做该做的事情。" ("In order to improve my depression, other people need to do the right things for me."), which was more semantically equivalent on the one hand and more culturally understandable and acceptable on the other hand.

In Item 11, "Whatever improvement" was translated into "什么程度的改善" ("To what extent (my depression) is improved") in Version 1 and "多多少少有了好转" ("more or less improvement") in Version 2, and "is largely a matter of good fortune" was translated into "很大程度上都纯属幸运" ("is largely a sheer matter of luck") in Version 1 and "那都是我走运" ("is completely attributable to my luck") in Version 2. To achieve better semantic equivalence, we decided to revise the Chinese wordings here to "我的抑郁症改善多少，主要看我运气好坏。" ("Whatever improvement occurs to my depression is mainly up to my luck."), which was believed to more cater to habitual wordings and to be more easily accepted in the Chinese cultural settings.

Item 13, "I deserve the credit when my depression improves and the blame when it gets worse.", was translated into "我的抑郁症病情好转归功于我自己，我的抑郁症病情恶化也怪我自己。" ("I deserve the credit when my depression improves, and I am to blame when it worsens.") in Version 1 and "我的抑郁症变好变坏都在我自己。" ("Whether my depression gets better or worse is entirely up to myself.") in Version 2. After panel discussions among all research members, we changed the translation of this item to "我自己决定了我的抑郁症变好还是变坏。" ("It is up to myself whether my depression gets better or worse."), which is more likely to meet the target Chinese readers' expectations that are shaped by their linguistic and cultural norms in the Chinese contexts.

Item 15, "it's a matter of fate" was translated into "那就是命运的问题了" ("it's a matter of fate") in Version 1 and "那就是我的命" ("that's my fate") in Version 2. After panel discussions, we changed these translations to "那就是命运的安排了" ("it's up to fate"), which was believed to be more natural and idiomatic and therefore more acceptable in expression than "那就是命运的问题了" and "那就是我的命" according to the Chinese audience's linguistic habits and cultural conceptions.

Item 18, "The type of help I receive from other people determines how soon my depression improves.", was translated into "我从其他人那里得到什么样的帮助决定了我的抑郁症病情好转的快慢。" ("The type of help I receive from other people determines how soon my condition improves.") in Version 1 and "别人给我的照顾多一些，我的抑郁症就好得快一些；别人给我的照顾少一些，我的抑郁症就好得慢一些。" ("When others care more for me, my depression gets better sooner; when others care less for me, my depression gets better later.") in Version 2. Based on panel discussions among all research members, we decided to revise the translation to "其他人给予我什么样的帮助决定了我的抑郁症好转的快慢。" ("The type of help

3.3 Results

other people give me determines how soon my depression improves."), which was thought to be more semantically equivalent to the original English Item but was not unanimously agreed upon among all research members. Due to the undetermined cultural comprehensibility of this translation, we decided to leave it to cognitive debriefing during pilot testing with a small number of target Chinese readers for final decision and revision.

Based on the discussion of the problematic translations of the items above, we reached a consensus on the translated version of the preliminary initial Chinese MHLC From C, as shown in Table 3.4. This version was pilot tested among a certain number of native Chinese patient participants in the following step of adaptation.

3.3.1.3 Pilot Testing of the Preliminary Initial Translated Chinese Version of the MHLC from C with a Chinese Sample: Cognitive Debriefing

During the pilot testing, the ten recruited native Chinese patient participants provided open feedback on whether and how they understood the translated and adapted scale. They raised some problems with the clarity and comprehensibility of the preliminary initial Chinese MHLC From C, although they believed that the whole translated scale was largely relevant to Chinese culture. In other words, there were not challenging questions and concepts irrelevant to Chinese culture (i.e., they were relevant to the participants' daily life), but there were issues of linguistic accessibility (i.e., they were unexpected or ambiguous to the participants) (Shan & Ji, 2023). Specifically, "病情" in some translated items is redundant according to colloquial Chinese expression; "那是命运的安排了" in translated Item 15 and "恶化" in some translated items still needs to be made more colloquial, understandable, and acceptable to Chinese readers, especially to those with low educational attainments; Item 12, "影响我抑郁症病情的主要因素是我自己的所作所为。", needs recasting in terms of the sequence of expression; Chinese expressions feature verbal phrases instead of nominal phrases, for example, "我自己行为" in translated Item 1 should be changed to "我自己怎么做"; some addition or deletions need to be made to make the translated items more culturally understandable and acceptable, for example, "我的抑郁症就顺其自然吧" in translated Item 2 should be changed to "我的抑郁症好转还是变坏就顺其自然吧"; etc. There were still more problems pointed out by the participants, which were rectified in Table 3.5.

Taking into consideration all comments and suggestions from the participants who took part in the cognitive debriefing, we not only improved the face validity (Shan & Ji, 2023) and the conceptual, semantic, and content equivalence (Sousa & Rojjanasrirat, 2011) but also further adjusted the structure of sentences used in the translated Chinese instrument, to make the final translated version easily understood by the target Chinese patient populations before psychometric testing (Sousa & Rojjanasrirat, 2011). As a result, all translated items were modified to varying degrees. The final version of the translated and adapted Chinese MHLC Form C is presented in Table 3.5.

Table 3.4 Preliminary initial Chinese MHLC Form C

编号	观念	非常不赞同	基本不赞同	有点不赞同	有点赞同	基本赞同	非常赞同
1	如果我的抑郁症病情恶化,我自己的行为决定了我多久会再次好转。	1	2	3	4	5	6
2	我的抑郁症病情就顺其自然吧。	1	2	3	4	5	6
3	如果我定期看病,我的抑郁症就不大会出问题。	1	2	3	4	5	6
4	大多数影响我抑郁症病情的因素都是偶然发生在我身上的。	1	2	3	4	5	6
5	每当我的抑郁症病情恶化时,我应该咨询受过医学培训的专业人士。	1	2	3	4	5	6
6	我的抑郁症病情好转还是恶化直接取决于我自己。	1	2	3	4	5	6
7	我的抑郁症病情是否好转、保持不变或者恶化,其他人起很大作用。	1	2	3	4	5	6
8	无论我的抑郁症病情出现什么样的恶化,都是我自己的问题。	1	2	3	4	5	6
9	我的抑郁症病情改善情况在很大程度上是由运气决定的。	1	2	3	4	5	6
10	要让我的抑郁症好转,其他人要为我做该做的事情。	1	2	3	4	5	6
11	我的抑郁症改善多少,主要看我运气好坏。	1	2	3	4	5	6
12	影响我抑郁症病情的主要因素是我自己的所作所为。	1	2	3	4	5	6
13	我自己决定我的抑郁症变好还是变坏。	1	2	3	4	5	6
14	遵从医嘱是防止我的抑郁症病情恶化的最好方法。	1	2	3	4	5	6
15	如果我的抑郁症恶化,那是命运的安排了。	1	2	3	4	5	6
16	如果我幸运的话,我的抑郁症病情会好转起来。	1	2	3	4	5	6
17	如果我的抑郁症病情恶化,那是因为我没有好好照顾自己。	1	2	3	4	5	6
18	其他人给予我什么样的帮助决定了我的抑郁症好转的快慢。	1	2	3	4	5	6

As Brislin (1980) observes, critical issues negatively impact many translation studies, even when certified translators are used. Our discussion above supports Brislin's (1980) observation. This is due primarily to three factors: (1) some translators' inadequate awareness of the rigorous translation requirements for cross-cultural studies; (2) their literal translation and insufficient emphasis on cultural nuances; and

3.3 Results

Table 3.5 Final version of the Chinese MHLC Form C which is glossed in English

编号	观念	非常不赞同	基本不赞同	有点不赞同	有点赞同	基本赞同	非常赞同
1	我的抑郁症要是加重的话，我自己怎么做决定了我好转的快慢。 **If my depression worsens, my own actions decide how soon it gets better**	1	2	3	4	5	6
2	我的抑郁症变好还是变坏都随它去吧。 **It is a natural course whether my depression gets better or worse**	1	2	3	4	5	6
3	我要是定期看病，我的抑郁症就不大会加重。 **If I treat my depression regularly, it is less likely to get worse**	1	2	3	4	5	6
4	大多数影响我抑郁症的原因都是碰巧发生在我身上的。 **Most causes of my depression happen to me by chance**	1	2	3	4	5	6
5	我的抑郁症每次加重时我都应该向医生咨询。 **Every time my depression worsens, I need to consult a doctor**	1	2	3	4	5	6

(continued)

Table 3.5 (continued)

编号	观念	非常不赞同	基本不赞同	有点不赞同	有点赞同	基本赞同	非常赞同
6	我自己直接影响我的抑郁症好转还是加重。 I myself directly make my depression better or worse	1	2	3	4	5	6
7	我的抑郁症好转、不发展还是加重, 别人起很大作用。 It is mainly up to others whether my depression gets better, unchanged, or worse	1	2	3	4	5	6
8	我的抑郁症加重到什么程度, 都是我自己造成的。 It is up to myself to what extent my depression worsens	1	2	3	4	5	6
9	我的抑郁症好转到什么程度主要看运气。 It is mainly up to luck to what extent my depression gets better	1	2	3	4	5	6
10	要让我的抑郁症好起来, 其他人要好好照顾我。 Others need to take good care of me to make my depression better and better	1	2	3	4	5	6

(continued)

3.3 Results

Table 3.5 (continued)

编号	观念	非常不赞同	基本不赞同	有点不赞同	有点赞同	基本赞同	非常赞同
11	我的抑郁症好转多少,主要看我运气好坏。 Whatever improvement happens to my depression is mainly up to my luck	1	2	3	4	5	6
12	我自己怎么做主要影响我抑郁症好转还是加重。 How I do largely decides whether my depression gets better or worse	1	2	3	4	5	6
13	我自己决定了我的抑郁症好转还是加重。 I decide whether my depression gets better or worse on my own	1	2	3	4	5	6
14	医生怎么说我就怎么做,是不让我的抑郁症加重的最好办法。 Doing whatever the doctor tells me is the best way to prevent my depression from worsening	1	2	3	4	5	6
15	万一我的抑郁症加重了,我就认命了。 In case my depression worsens, it is my fate	1	2	3	4	5	6

(continued)

Table 3.5 (continued)

编号	观念	非常不赞同	基本不赞同	有点不赞同	有点赞同	基本赞同	非常赞同
16	我要是运气好的话,我的抑郁症会好起来。 If I'm lucky, my depression will get better and better	1	2	3	4	5	6
17	我的抑郁症要是加重的话,那是因为我没有照顾好自己。 It is because I do not take good care of myself that my depression gets worse	1	2	3	4	5	6
18	其他人把我照顾得好,我的抑郁症好的就快;其他人把我照顾得不好,我的抑郁症好的就慢。 If others take good care of me, my depression will get better sooner; if others do not take good care of me, my depression will get better later	1	2	3	4	5	6

(3) challenges posed by colloquial expressions, slang and jargon, idiomatic phrases, and emotionally evocative words (Sperber, 2004). Through the three steps of translation and adaptation above, we managed to generate the final version of the Chinese MHLC Form C, which we made maximally relevant, understandable, and acceptable to Chinese readers in the Chinese cultural contexts to the maximum of our potential. This version was then used to classify Chinese patients into different clusters and to identify associated factors.

3.3.2 Using the Chinese MHLC Form C to Classify Patients and Identifying Factors Associated with Low Self-efficacy

3.3.2.1 Descriptive Statistics

Table 3.6 presents the descriptive statistics of the data collected from the patient participants. All data in the 988 returned questionnaires were valid. The patients had a mean age of 42.85 (SD = 11.544) years. 45% (n = 443) of them were men. The mean score for education was 3.21 (SD = 1.474), showing that their average educational level was between Year 12 and diploma. The mean score for their self-reported disease knowledge was 2.42, indicating that they thought that their knowledge of disease was between 'a lot' and 'some.' The mean scores of the three functional items on the AAHLS scale were 2.06 (SD = 0.735), 2.13 (SD = 0.969), and 2.09 (SD = 0.741), respectively. These mean scores indicate that they 'sometimes' needed help to read and comprehend health information and complete official documents and were 'sometimes' able to identify and secure others' help. The mean scores of the three communicative items on the AAHLS scale were 1.74 (SD = 0.754), 1.87 (SD = 0.745), and 1.88 (SD = 0.744), respectively. These mean scores indicate that when they talked to a doctor or nurse, they 'often' or 'sometimes' gave them all the information they needed, they 'often' or 'sometimes' asked the questions they needed to ask, and they 'often' or 'sometimes' made sure they explained anything that they did not understand. The mean scores of Items 1–5 on the critical health literacy subscale of the AAHLS scale were 1.97 (SD = 0.752), 1.94 (SD = 0.728), 1.91 (SD = 0.746), 2.01 (SD = 0.730), 1.97 (SD = 0.734), and 1.56 (SD = 0.496), respectively. These mean scores indicate that they 'sometimes' found out lots of different information about their health, they 'sometimes' thought carefully about whether health information made sense in their particular situation, they 'sometimes' tried to work out whether information about their health could be trusted, they 'sometimes' questioned their doctor or nurse's advice based on their own research, they 'sometimes' thought that there were plenty of ways to have a say in what the government did about health, and they were inclined to believe that "good housing, education, decent jobs, and good local facilities" mattered most for their health. The scores for the 8 items on the eHEALS ranged from 2.83 (SD = 1.174) to 2.96 (SD = 1.179), indicating their uncertainty about their skills to use eHealth resources and interventions. The mean score for each item on the GHNT scale was 1.56 (SD = 0.497), 1.18 (SD = 0.383), 1.21 (SD = 0.406), 1.93 (SD = 0.333), 1.84 (SD = 0.370), and 1.77 (SD = 0.420), showing that a large proportion of participants answered the 6 questions on the GHNT scale incorrectly, especially questions 1 (551/988, 55.8%), 4 (908/988, 91.9%), 5 (826/988, 83.6%), and 6 (763/988, 77.2%). As with their scoring performance on the Multidimensional Health Locus of Control (MHLC) Scales (MHLC) Form C, they averagely scored 18.21 (SD = 4.790), 16.87 (SD = 4.803), 10.36 (SD = 3.5393), and 8.44 (SD = 2.915) on the 'Internal,' 'Chance,' 'Doctor,' and 'Powerful Others' subscales, respectively. The determined response of 'slightly disagree' for the 'Internal' subscale indicates that they somehow did not believe in their internal drives to maintain healthy. The determined response between 'moderately disagree' and 'slightly disagree' for the 'Chance' subscale implies that they were generally less likely to attribute their health to a matter of chance. The determined response between 'slightly disagree' and 'slightly agree' for the 'Doctor' subscale means that they were generally uncertain about the role of doctors in the maintenance of their own health. The determined response between 'moderately disagree' and 'slightly disagree' for the 'Powerful Others' subscale means that they generally did nor believe in the role of others in the maintenance of their own health.

3.3.2.2 Model Fit Statistics

Table 3.7 and Fig. 3.1 shows the model fit statistics of the latent class analysis. The Akaike information criterion (AIC) and the Bayesian information criterion (BIC) provide measures of model performance. Smaller AIC and BIC are indicative of better model performance. Indexes like the Lo-Mendell-Rubin likelihood (LL) ratio test, and the bootstrap likelihood ratio test examined whether adding clusters would significantly improve model performance. We took into consideration all the factors and decided to opt for a 2-cluster solution for better model performance and simplicity to guide the subsequent qualitative analyses, as shown in Table 3.8.

3.3.2.3 Profiling of 2 Latent Clusters

Cluster 1—Low Self-efficacy Group

Patient participants in Cluster 1 had low (9–18) to medium scores (19–27) on the 'Internal' sub-scale (with conditional probabilities higher than 0.5 until the internal sum score of 27), suggesting a mix of a less inclination and a slight inclination to believe in their own capability to manage self-health. For example, they were more likely to 'strongly disagree' (coding 1), 'moderately disagree' (coding 2), 'slightly disagree' (coding 3), or 'slightly agree' (coding 4) with statements such as 'If my depression worsens, it is my own behavior which determines how soon I will feel better again' (Item 1 on the Chinese depression-specific MHLC Form C), 'I am directly responsible for my depression getting better or worse' (Item 6 on the Chinese depression-specific MHLC Form C), and 'Whatever goes wrong with my depression is my own fault' (Item 8 on the Chinese depression-specific MHLC Form C).

Patients in Cluster 1 also had low (4–9) to medium scores (10–13) on the 'Doctor' sub-scale (with conditional probabilities higher than 0.5 until the internal sum score of 13), suggesting that they had limited trust in medical and health professionals and the health benefits of adhering to their recommendations and advice. For example, they were more likely to 'strongly disagree' (coding 1), 'moderately disagree' (coding 2), 'slightly disagree' (coding 3), or 'slightly agree' (coding 4) with statements such

3.3 Results

Table 3.6 Descriptive statistics of the data collected (N = 988)

	Minimum	Maximum	Mean	Std. deviation
Age	17	68	42.85	11.544
Gender	N/A[a]	N/A	N/A	N/A
Education	1	6	3.21	1.474
Disease knowledge	1	4	2.42	0.958
FUHL1[b]	1	3	2.06	0.735
FUHL2[c]	1	4	2.13	0.969
FUHL3[d]	1	3	2.09	0.741
COHL1[e]	1	3	1.74	0.754
COHL2[f]	1	3	1.87	0.745
COHL3[g]	1	3	1.88	0.744
CRHL1[h]	1	3	1.97	0.752
CRHL2[i]	1	3	1.94	0.728
CRHL3[j]	1	3	1.91	0.746
CRHL4[k]	1	3	2.01	0.730
CRHL5[l]	1	3	1.97	0.734
CRHL6[m]	1	2	1.56	0.469
eHL1[n]	1	5	2.83	1.176
eHL2[o]	1	5	2.86	1.197
eHL3[p]	1	5	2.83	1.174
eHL4[q]	1	5	2.96	1.179
eHL5[r]	1	5	2.85	1.203
eHL6[s]	1	5	2.88	1.199
eHL7[t]	1	5	2.93	1.190
eHL8[u]	1	5	2.87	1.204
GHNT1[v]	1	2	1.56	0.497
GHNT2[w]	1	2	1.18	0.383
GHNT3[x]	1	2	1.21	0.406
GHNT4[y]	1	2	1.93	0.333
GHNT5[z]	1	2	1.84	0.370
GHNT6[aa]	1	2	1.77	0.420
Internal scale[ab]	6	36	18.21	4.789
Chance scale[ac]	6	36	16.87	4.803
Doctor scale[ad]	3	18	10.36	3.539

(continued)

Table 3.6 (continued)

	Minimum	Maximum	Mean	Std. deviation
OtherPeople_Scale[ae]	3	18	8.44	2.915

[a] Not applicable
[b] Functional Health Literacy Item 1: How often do you need someone to help you when you are given information to read by your physician, nurse, or pharmacist?
[c] Functional Health Literacy Item 2: When you need help, can you easily get someone to assist you? 3.04 (0.9; 1–4)
[d] Functional Health Literacy Item 3: Do you need help to fill in official documents?
[e] Communicative Health Literacy Item 1: When you talk to a physician or nurse, do you give them all the information they need to help you?
[f] Communicative Health Literacy Item 2: When you talk to a physician or nurse, do you ask the questions you need to ask?
[g] Communicative Health Literacy Item 3: When you talk to a physician or nurse, do you ensure they explain anything that you do not understand?
[h] Critical Health Literacy Item 1: Are you someone who likes to find out lots of different information about your health?
[i] Critical Health Literacy Item 2: How often do you think carefully about whether health information makes sense in your particular situation?
[j] Critical Health Literacy Item 3: How often do you try to work out whether information about your health can be trusted?
[k] Critical Health Literacy Item 4: Are you the sort of person who might question your doctor or nurse's advice based on your own research?
[la] Critical Health Literacy Item 5: Do you think that there plenty of ways to have a say in what the government does about health?
[m] Critical Health Literacy Item 6: What do you think matters most for everyone's health? a) information and encouragement to lead healthy lifestyles; b) good housing, education, decent jobs and good local facilities
[n] eHealth Literacy Item 1: I know what health resources are available on the Internet
[o] eHealth Literacy Item 2: I know where to find helpful health resources on the Internet
[p] eHealth Literacy Item 3: I know how to find helpful health resources on the Internet
[q] eHealth Literacy Item 4: I know how to use the Internet to answer my health questions
[r] eHealth Literacy Item 5: I know how to use the health information I find on the Internet to help me
[s] eHealth Literacy Item 6: I have the skills I need to evaluate the health resources I find on the Internet
[t] eHealth Literacy Item 7: I can tell high quality from low-quality health resources on the Internet
[u] eHealth Literacy Item 8: I feel confident using information from the Internet to make health decisions
[v] General Health Numeracy Test Item 1: Call your physician if you have a temperature of 100.4 °F or greater. The thermometer looks like the following: 100.2 F: Do you call a physician?
[w] General Health Numeracy Test Item 2: If 4 people out of 20 have a chance of getting a cold, what would be the risk of getting a cold?
[x] General Health Numeracy Test Item 3: Suppose that the maximum heart rate for a 60 year old woman is 160 beats per minute and that she is told to exercise at 80% of her maximum heart rate. What is 80% of that woman's maximum heart rate?
[y] General Health Numeracy Test Item 4: You ate half the container of carrots. How many grams of carbohydrate did you eat?
[z] General Health Numeracy Test Item 5: Your doctor tells you that you have high cholesterol. He informs you that you have a 10% risk of having a heart attack in the next 5 years. If you start on a cholesterol-lowering drug, you can reduce your risk by 30%. What is your 5-year risk if you take the drug?
[aa] General Health Numeracy Test Item 6: A mammogram is used to screen women for breast cancer. False positives are tests that incorrectly show a positive result. 85% of positive mammograms are actually false positives. If 1000 women receive mammograms, and 200 are told there is an abnormal finding, how many women are likely to actually have breast cancer?
[ab] The Internal Locus of Control: beliefs that one's health is up to their own actions and behaviors
[ac] The Chance Locus of Control: beliefs that one's health is up to fate, chance, or luck
[ad] The Doctor Locus of Control: beliefs that one's health is up to doctors
[ae] The Powerful Others Locus of Control: beliefs that one's health is up to others' actions and behaviors

3.3 Results

Table 3.7 Model fit statistics for male data

Models	BIC (LL)	AIC (LL)	AIC3 (LL)	LL	Npar[a]	Max. BVR[b]	Class. Err	Entropy R^{2}[c]
1-Cluster	70,525.3587	70,163.0782	70,237.0782	−35,007.5391	74	340.5345	0	1
2-Cluster	67,436.3732	66,687.3338	66,840.3338	−33,190.6669	153	168.2452	0.0088	0.9639
3-Cluster	66,827.4553	65,691.6569	65,923.6569	−32,613.8284	232	145.294	0.0113	0.9649
4-Cluster	66,781.7713	65,259.214	65,570.214	−32,318.607	311	142.0332	0.0109	0.9712
5-Cluster	66,884.9483	64,975.632	65,365.632	−32,097.816	390	74.2235	0.0314	0.9206
6-Cluster	67,158.0984	64,862.0232	65,331.0232	−31,962.0116	469	71.2239	0.0262	0.9339

[a] BVR: bivariate residual
[b] Npar: number of estimated parameters
[c] Entropy R^2: Values > 0.8 indicate high degree of separation between classes

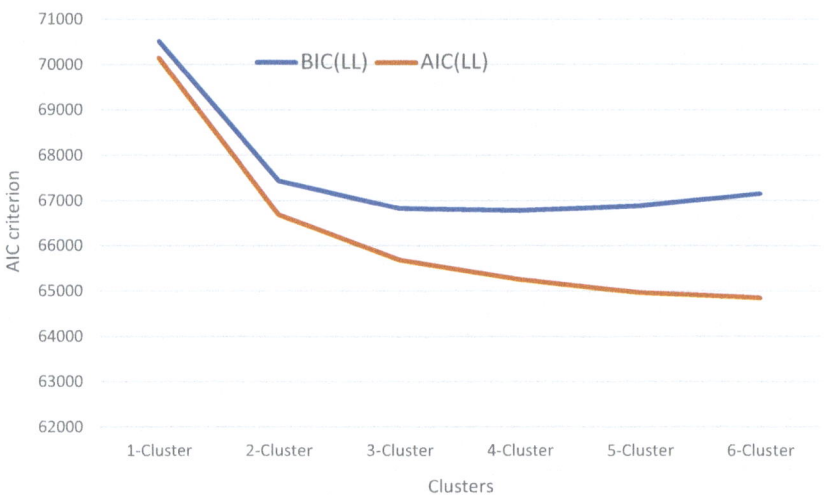

Fig. 3.1 Model fit statistics changes. AIC: Akaike information criterion. BIC: Bayesian information criterion. LL: Lo-Mendell-Rubin likelihood

as 'If I see my doctor regularly, I am less likely to have problems with my depression' (Item 3 on the Chinese depression-specific MHLC Form C).

Patients in Cluster 1 had more spread scores across the 'Other People' sub-scale ranging from 4 to 18, suggesting that while some patients in Cluster 1 were unlikely to see the influence of others' behaviors on their own health as significant, other patients in this cluster were likely to see the influence of others' behaviors on their own health as significant. For example, patients in this cluster were likely to 'strongly disagree' (coding 1), 'moderately disagree' (coding 2), 'slightly disagree' (coding 3), 'slightly agree' (coding 4), 'moderately agree' (coding 5), or 'strongly agree' (coding 6) with statements such as 'Other people play a big role in whether my condition improves, stays the same, or gets worse' (Item 7 on the Chinese depression-specific MHLC Form C), 'In order for my condition to improve, it is up to other people to see that the right things happen' (Item 10 on the Chinese depression-specific MHLC Form C), and 'The type of help I receive from other people determines how soon my condition improves' (Item 18 on the Chinese depression-specific MHLC Form C).

Patients in Cluster 1 had low (11–18) to medium scores (19–28) on the 'Chance' sub-scale, suggesting that while some people in this cluster did not believe in the role of luck in one's health management, others did 'slightly' agree with statements, such as 'As to my condition, what will be will be' (Item 2 on the Chinese depression-specific MHLC Form C), 'Most things that affect my condition happen to me by chance' (Item 4 on the Chinese depression-specific MHLC Form C), 'Luck plays a big part in determining how my condition improves' (Item 9 on the Chinese depression-specific MHLC Form C), 'Whatever improvement occurs with my condition is largely a matter of good fortune' (Item 11 on the Chinese depression-specific MHLC Form

3.3 Results

Table 3.8 Posterior probabilities of response across latent clusters

Posterior probabilities	Cluster 1	Cluster 2	Total probability
Cluster size	0.7246	0.2754	1
Internal_Scale (Median = 18)			
6	0.1481	0.8519	1
8	0	1	1
9	0.5007	0.4993	1
10	0.578	0.422	1
11	0.7135	0.2865	1
12	0.743	0.257	1
13	0.8233	0.1767	1
14	0.7911	0.2089	1
15	0.9655	0.0345	1
16	0.8472	0.1528	1
17	0.8368	0.1632	1
18	0.7218	0.2782	1
19	0.8246	0.1754	1
20	0.7328	0.2672	1
21	0.7109	0.2891	1
22	0.6405	0.3595	1
23	0.6625	0.3375	1
24	0.4502	0.5498	1
25	0.5007	0.4993	1
26	0.6836	0.3164	1
27	0.6664	0.3336	1
28	0.336	0.664	1
29	0.2036	0.7964	1
30	0.1998	0.8002	1
31	0	1	1
32	0	1	1
34	0	1	1
35	1	0	1
36	1	0	1
Chance_Scale (Median = 18)			
6	0.0769	0.9231	1
7	0.1293	0.8707	1
8	0.1552	0.8448	1
9	0.0777	0.9223	1
10	0.4763	0.5237	1

(continued)

Table 3.8 (continued)

Posterior probabilities	Cluster 1	Cluster 2	Total probability
11	0.5758	0.4242	1
12	0.6785	0.3215	1
13	0.7947	0.2053	1
14	0.754	0.246	1
15	0.798	0.202	1
16	0.8501	0.1499	1
17	0.9205	0.0795	1
18	0.6991	0.3009	1
19	0.7481	0.2519	1
20	0.7494	0.2506	1
21	0.7867	0.2133	1
22	0.7574	0.2426	1
23	0.8434	0.1566	1
24	0.5428	0.4572	1
25	0.8753	0.1247	1
26	0.9088	0.0912	1
27	0.7481	0.2519	1
28	1	0	1
29	0.3331	0.6669	1
30	0.1971	0.8029	1
36	1	0	1
Doctors_Scale (Median = 9)			
3	0.3454	0.6546	1
4	0.8571	0.1429	1
5	0.9736	0.0264	1
6	0.9677	0.0323	1
7	0.9482	0.0518	1
8	0.9713	0.0287	1
9	0.8435	0.1565	1
10	0.8017	0.1983	1
11	0.8034	0.1966	1
12	0.5341	0.4659	1
13	0.6462	0.3538	1
14	0.4176	0.5824	1
15	0.2269	0.7731	1
16	0.2492	0.7508	1
17	0.3189	0.6811	1

(continued)

3.3 Results

Table 3.8 (continued)

Posterior probabilities	Cluster 1	Cluster 2	Total probability
18	0.2692	0.7308	1
Other_People_Scale (Median = 9)			
3	0.2614	0.7386	1
4	0.6168	0.3832	1
5	0.6672	0.3328	1
6	0.7191	0.2809	1
7	0.771	0.229	1
8	0.8296	0.1704	1
9	0.6237	0.3763	1
10	0.8049	0.1951	1
11	0.8033	0.1967	1
12	0.7288	0.2712	1
13	0.7994	0.2006	1
14	0.8112	0.1888	1
15	0.588	0.412	1
16	1	0	1
17	1	0	1
18	1	0	1

C), 'If my condition worsens, it's a matter of fate' (Item 15 on the Chinese depression-specific MHLC Form C), and 'If I am lucky, my condition will get better' (Item 16 on the Chinese depression-specific MHLC Form C).

Cluster 2—Moderate Self-efficacy Group

Patients in Cluster 2 showed two scenarios. Some had high scores on the 'Internal' sub-scale ranging from 28 to 34, suggesting that they had stronger beliefs in their own capability to manage their health. Their responses to the questions of the 'Internal' scale were more likely to be 'slightly agree,' 'moderately agree,' or 'strongly agree' with statements of the Chinese depression-specific MHLC Form C stressing the importance of self-discipline and self-management to achieve optimal health outcomes when it comes to the prevention and treatment of depression. For example, people in Cluster 2 were agreeable with statements like 'the main thing which affects my condition is what I myself do' (Item 12 on the Chinese depression-specific MHLC Form C), 'I deserve the credit when my condition improves and the blame when it gets worse' (Item 13 on the Chinese depression-specific MHLC Form C), and 'If my condition takes a turn for the worse, it is because I have not been taking proper care of myself'(Item 17 on the Chinese depression-specific MHLC Form C). In contrast, other patients had low scores on the 'Internal' sub-scale ranging from 6 to 8, suggesting that they were more likely to 'strongly disagree' with statements of the Chinese depression-specific MHLC Form C stressing the importance of self-discipline and self-management to achieve optimal health outcomes when it comes to the prevention and treatment of depression.

Patients in Cluster 2 also displayed two scenarios. Some had higher scores on the 'Doctor' sub-scale, ranging from 14 to 18, suggesting that they had moderate to high levels of trust in health and medical professionals and the importance of adherence to their advice to achieve better health outcomes. Their responses to the questions of the 'Doctor' sub-scale were more likely to be 'moderately agree' or 'strongly agree' with statements of the Chinese depression-specific MHLC Form C highlighting the importance of seeking medical support to prevent, diagnose, and treat depression. For example, 'whenever my condition worsens, I should consult a medically trained professional.' (Item 5 on the Chinese depression-specific MHLC Form C), 'Following doctor's orders to the letter is the best way to keep my condition from getting any worse' (Item 14 on the Chinese depression-specific MHLC Form C). By contrast, other patients had the lowest score of 3 on the 'Doctor' sub-scale, suggesting that they had the lowest level of trust in health and medical professionals and the importance of adherence to their advice to achieve better health outcomes. Their responses to the questions of the 'Doctor' sub-scale were more likely to be 'strongly disagree' with statements of the Chinese depression-specific MHLC Form C highlighting the importance of seeking medical support to prevent, diagnose, and treat depression.

Patients in Cluster 2 had a very high score (3) on the 'Other People' sub-scale, suggesting that all of them were more unlikely to associate their own depression outcomes with other people in their lives.

Chinese participants in Cluster 2 were divided on the 'Chance' sub-scale, with some people having very low scores (6–10) and others having very high scores (29–30). It indicates that a polarized view regarding the role of chance in their health and well-being existed among this group of patients, in a similar way that a polarized view was displayed on the role of internal motivations and doctors in terms of the prevention and treatment of depression.

Table 3.9 shows descriptive statistics of the two latent clusters representing the two levels of self-efficacy among the study participants. The low self-efficacy group (Cluster 1, n = 716) represented 72.5% (716/988) of the total sample. They had an average mean of 17.79 (SD = 1.44) on the 'Internal' scale, an average mean of 17.67 (SD = 0.15) on the 'Chance' scale, an average mean of 9.13 (SD = 0.10) on the 'Doctor' scale, and an average mean of 8.76 (SD = 0.10) on the 'Other People' scale. The moderate self-efficacy group (Cluster 2, n = 272) represented 27.5% (272/988) of the total sample. They had an average mean of 19.50 (SD = 4.23) on the internal scale, an average mean of 14.37 (SD = 0.39) on the 'Chance' scale, an average mean 14.23 (SD = 0.18) on the 'Doctor' scale, and an average mean 7.43 (SD = 0.24) on the 'Other People' scale

Next, we compared the differences between the two clusters across the four sub-scales. The result of the Welch Test in Table 3.10 shows that there were statistically significant differences among the two clusters representing two distinct levels of

3.3 Results

Table 3.9 Descriptive statistics of the latent clusters

Sub-scales	Cluster			Statistic	Std. error
Internal	1	Mean		17.7944	0.1443
		95% confidence interval for mean	Lower bound	17.5111	
			Upper bound	18.0777	
		5% trimmed mean		17.7425	
		Median		18	
		Variance		15.597	
		Std. deviation		3.94927	
		Minimum		6	
		Maximum		36	
		Range		30	
		Interquartile range		5	
		Skewness		0.259	0.089
		Kurtosis		0.609	0.178
	2	Mean		19.5021	0.42861
		95% confidence interval for mean	Lower bound	18.6577	
			Upper bound	20.3465	
		5% trimmed mean		19.6086	
		Median		21	
		Variance		43.907	
		Std. deviation		6.6262	
		Minimum		6	
		Maximum		34	
		Range		28	
		Interquartile range		10	
		Skewness		− 0.34	0.157
		Kurtosis		− 0.527	0.314
Chance	1	Mean		17.67	0.146
		95% confidence interval for mean	Lower bound	17.38	
			Upper bound	17.95	
		5% trimmed mean		17.6	
		Median		17	
		Variance		15.995	
		Std. deviation		3.999	
		Minimum		6	
		Maximum		36	
		Range		30	
		Interquartile range		5	

(continued)

Table 3.9 (continued)

Sub-scales	Cluster			Statistic	Std. error
		Skewness		0.283	0.089
		Kurtosis		0.262	0.178
	2	Mean		14.37	0.394
		95% confidence interval for mean	Lower bound	13.59	
			Upper bound	15.14	
		5% trimmed mean		14.09	
		Median		14	
		Variance		37.108	
		Std. deviation		6.092	
		Minimum		6	
		Maximum		30	
		Range		24	
		Interquartile range		10	
		Skewness		0.427	0.157
		Kurtosis		−0.518	0.314
Doctors	1	Mean		9.13	0.102
		95% confidence interval for mean	Lower bound	8.93	
			Upper bound	9.33	
		5% trimmed mean		9.03	
		Median		9	
		Variance		7.796	
		Std. deviation		2.792	
		Minimum		3	
		Maximum		18	
		Range		15	
		Interquartile range		4	
		Skewness		0.552	0.089
		Kurtosis		0.297	0.178
	2	Mean		14.23	0.178
		95% confidence interval for mean	Lower bound	13.88	
			Upper bound	14.59	
		5% trimmed mean		14.48	
		Median		15	
		Variance		7.6	
		Std. deviation		2.757	
		Minimum		3	
		Maximum		18	

(continued)

3.3 Results

Table 3.9 (continued)

Sub-scales	Cluster			Statistic	Std. error
		Range		15	
		Interquartile range		3	
		Skewness		−1.644	0.157
		Kurtosis		4.563	0.314
Other People	1	Mean		8.76	0.101
		95% confidence interval for mean	Lower bound	8.56	
			Upper bound	8.96	
		5% trimmed mean		8.71	
		Median		9	
		Variance		7.632	
		Std. deviation		2.763	
		Minimum		3	
		Maximum		18	
		Range		15	
		Interquartile range		4	
		Skewness		0.273	0.089
		Kurtosis		−0.224	0.178
	2	Mean		7.43	0.204
		95% confidence interval for mean	Lower bound	7.03	
			Upper bound	7.83	
		5% trimmed mean		7.29	
		Median		7	
		Variance		9.901	
		Std. deviation		3.147	
		Minimum		3	
		Maximum		15	
		Range		12	
		Interquartile range		4	
		Skewness		0.342	0.157
		Kurtosis		−0.519	0.314

self-efficacy among the study participants in their scores on the 'Internal,' 'Chance,' 'Doctor,' and 'Other People' sub-scales.

Table 3.10 Robust tests of equality of means (welch test)

	Statistic	df1	df2	Sig
Internal scale	14.258	1	293.811	< 0.001
Chance scale	61.635	1	306.13	< 0.001
Doctor scale	617.695	1	405.482	< 0.001
Other people scale	34.419	1	362.499	< 0.001

3.3.2.4 Factors Associated with the Low Self-efficacy

Table 3.11 shows that the conditional probabilities of all variables within the 2 identified clusters of self-efficacy. From these conditional probabilities, Cluster 1, the low self-efficacy subgroup of patient participants were found to be closely associated with particular factors to be presented below.

Older Age

Table 3.11 shows that the conditional probabilities of age groups within the 2 identified clusters of self-efficacy. From this table, patients of low self-efficacy were more likely to be averagely aged 45.7 years old. In contrast, patients of moderate self-efficacy were more likely to be averagely aged 35.5 years old.

Male Sex

Table 3.11 shows that the conditional probabilities of genders within the 2 identified clusters of self-efficacy. As can be seen, 51.3% of the low-efficacy cluster were men, compared with 72.2% of the moderate-efficacy cluster being women.

Limited Educational Attainment

Table 3.11 shows that the conditional probabilities of different levels of educational attainment within the 2 identified clusters of self-efficacy. It can be seen that patients of low self-efficacy were more likely to have lower levels of education (Year 6 to Year 12). In contrast, patients of moderate self-efficacy were more likely to have adequate to high educational levels (diploma, university graduate, postgraduate or above).

Higher Level of Self-reported Disease Knowledge

Table 3.11 shows that the conditional probabilities of different levels of self-reported disease knowledge within the 2 identified clusters of self-efficacy. It is clear that just below 60% of patient participants of the low self-efficacy cluster were more likely to report knowing 'very well' or 'a lot' about diseases. In contrast, over 60% of patients of the moderate self-efficacy cluster were more likely to report knowing 'some' or 'very limited' about diseases.

3.3 Results

Table 3.11 Conditional probabilities of all variables within each cluster

Conditional probabilities	Cluster 1	Cluster 2
Cluster size	0.7246	0.2754
Age		
Mean	45.6543	35.4513
Gender		
Male	0.513	0.2783
Female	0.487	0.7217
Total probability	1	1
Education		
Year 6	0.1828	0.0224
Year 9	0.2905	0.1141
Year 12	0.2225	0.0797
Diploma	0.1992	0.1889
University graduate	0.0938	0.4331
Postgraduate or above	0.0112	0.1617
Total probability	1	1
Disease knowledge		
Very well	0.2574	0.0579
A lot	0.3303	0.2445
Some	0.2542	0.6287
Very limited	0.1582	0.0689
FUHL1		
Often	0.2889	0.1218
Sometimes	0.4089	0.5817
Rarely	0.3022	0.2965
FUHL2		
Often	0.2402	0.4229
Sometimes	0.3734	0.4987
Rarely	0.2235	0.0662
Not applicable	0.1629	0.0123
FUHL3		
Often	0.2842	0.1048
Sometimes	0.4128	0.5273
Rarely	0.303	0.3679
COHL1		
Often	0.3449	0.7135
Sometimes	0.4047	0.2619
Rarely	0.2504	0.0247
COHL2		

(continued)

Table 3.11 (continued)

Conditional probabilities	Cluster 1	Cluster 2
Often	0.3031	0.4667
Sometimes	0.4165	0.4624
Rarely	0.2804	0.0708
COHL3		
Often	0.306	0.4519
Sometimes	0.4199	0.461
Rarely	0.2742	0.0872
CRHL1		
Often	0.2862	0.3348
Sometimes	0.404	0.5136
Rarely	0.3097	0.1516
CRHL2		
Often	0.3023	0.2778
Sometimes	0.4032	0.6372
Rarely	0.2945	0.085
CRHL3		
Yes	0.311	0.3614
Maybe	0.3842	0.5733
No	0.3048	0.0653
CRHL4		
Yes	0.3179	0.1118
Maybe	0.4039	0.6353
No	0.2782	0.253
CRHL5		
Yes	0.3241	0.1799
Maybe	0.4008	0.6177
No	0.2751	0.2024
CRHL6		
Quality health information	0.3825	0.5776
Better living conditions	0.6175	0.4224
eHEAL1		
Strongly disagree	0.2192	0.0003
Disagree	0.2956	0.0453
Neutral	0.2572	0.5214
Agree	0.1117	0.419
Strongly agree	0.1162	0.0139
eHEAL2		
Strongly disagree	0.2205	0.0078

(continued)

3.3 Results

Table 3.11 (continued)

Conditional probabilities	Cluster 1	Cluster 2
Disagree	0.279	0.023
Neutral	0.2719	0.5123
Agree	0.0968	0.4363
Strongly agree	0.1318	0.0206
eHEAL3		
Strongly disagree	0.2094	0.0003
Disagree	0.3273	0.0173
Neutral	0.241	0.5126
Agree	0.1065	0.4549
Strongly agree	0.1158	0.015
eHEAL4		
Strongly disagree	0.1718	0.0075
Disagree	0.2874	0.0597
Neutral	0.2449	0.5062
Agree	0.1484	0.4182
Strongly agree	0.1476	0.0084
eHEAL5		
Strongly disagree	0.2345	0.0004
Disagree	0.2861	0.0447
Neutral	0.2428	0.4051
Agree	0.1253	0.5452
Strongly agree	0.1114	0.0047
eHEAL6		
Strongly disagree	0.219	0.008
Disagree	0.2542	0.0772
Neutral	0.2715	0.4323
Agree	0.1325	0.4637
Strongly agree	0.1228	0.0188
eHEAL7		
Strongly disagree	0.1885	0.0003
Disagree	0.3113	0.0336
Neutral	0.2462	0.4182
Agree	0.1254	0.5191
Strongly agree	0.1287	0.0288
eHEAL8		
Strongly disagree	0.1963	0.0127
Disagree	0.3095	0.1156
Neutral	0.2248	0.4559

(continued)

Table 3.11 (continued)

Conditional probabilities	Cluster 1	Cluster 2
Agree	0.1242	0.4156
Strongly agree	0.1452	0.0002
GHNT1		
Correct	0.4409	0.4461
Wrong	0.5591	0.5539
GHNT2		
Correct	0.8992	0.6184
Wrong	0.1008	0.3816
GHNT3		
Correct	0.8855	0.5477
Wrong	0.1145	0.4523
GHNT4		
Correct	0.0461	0.169
Wrong	0.9539	0.8273
GHNT5		
Correct	0.0947	0.3462
Wrong	0.9053	0.6538
GHNT6		
Correct	0.1153	0.5235
Wrong	0.8847	0.4765

Limited Functional Health Literacy

From Table 3.11, over 70% of patients of the low self-efficacy cluster were more likely to 'often' or 'sometimes' need help to read and comprehend health information and complete official documents, and over 60% of patients of this cluster were more like to be 'often' or 'sometimes' unable to identify and secure others' help. In contrast, over 90% of patients of the high self-efficacy cluster were more likely to 'sometimes' or 'rarely' need help to read and comprehend health information and complete official documents, and were more likely to be 'often' or 'sometimes' able to identify and secure others' help.

Limited Communicative Health Literacy

Table 3.11 shows that around about 70% of patients of low self-efficacy versus over 90% of patients of moderate self-efficacy were more likely to 'often' or 'sometimes' give a doctor or nurse all the information they needed, 'often' or 'sometimes' ask the questions they needed to ask, and 'often' or 'sometimes' make sure a doctor or nurse explained anything that they did not understand when they talked to a doctor or nurse.

Limited Critical Health Literacy

It can be seen from Table 3.11 that 62% of patients of the low-efficacy cluster were inclined to believe that good housing, education, decent jobs, and good local facilities mattered most for their health while 58% of patients of the moderate-efficacy cluster were more likely to consider that quality Health Information mattered most for their health condition.

Limited Digital Health Literacy

Table 3.11 shows that around 50% of patients of low self-efficacy were less likely to know where to find useful information on the internet, to know the means and methods to identify useful health information on the internet, and to agree that they had the skills and knowledge that enabled them to navigate electronic health platforms and find helpful health-related information. In contrast, approximately 40–50% of patients of adequate self-efficacy were more likely to agree or strongly agree that they were equipped with such essential skills and knowledge.

Limited Health Numeracy Literacy

Table 3.11 shows that 88.5% of patients of the low self-efficacy cluster answered question 6 on the GHNT scale incorrectly while 52.4% patients of the adequate self-efficacy cluster answered this question correctly.

3.4 Discussion

3.4.1 Principal Findings

3.4.1.1 Translation and Adaptation of the Chinese MHLC Form C

While it is extremely challenging to make a translated instrument culturally relevant, comprehensible, and acceptable to the target readers, we successfully translated and adapted the MHLC Form C into a depression-specific Chinese version which we believed to display a high degree of relevance, comprehensibility, and acceptability in the context of Chinese culture. A total of three steps adopted in the entire translation and adaptation process ensured the semantic equivalence and cultural appropriateness of the Chinese MHLC Form C, including (1) independently translating the original English MHLC Form C by two bilingual and bi-cultural translators whose native language is Chinese, (2) comparing not only the two independent translated versions but also these two version with the original English MHLC Form C to decide on the preliminary initial translated version, and (3) improving the preliminary initial translated version through cognitive debriefing through pilot testing it with a small numbers of participants.

Choosing qualified bilingual and bi-cultural translators whose mother tongue is the target language is the prerequisite for quality translation of an instrument. Before selecting competent translators in this study, we fully considered the fact that qualified translators are not always sufficiently knowledgeable in specialized subject areas related to some scales and are frequently unable to translate the content area of medical materials (Maneesriwongul & Dixon, 2004). One translator (Meng Ji) we used is a competent bilingual and bi-cultural translator who is a native Chinese speaker who has been living in Australia for many years and who has relatively rich experience in engaging in the translation and translation studies of health and medical materials, therefore largely warranting the quality of the original English MHLC Form C into Chinese. Another translator (Yi Shan) is also a competent bilingual and bi-cultural translator who is also a native Chinese speaker but who hasn't lived in an English-speaking country for a long time and accumulated adequate experience in engaging in the translation and translation studies of health and medical materials. Yi Shan's relatively less adapted translation of the original English MHLC Form C confirms the importance of sufficient knowledge about specialized subject areas related to the scale to be translated.

Regardless of the competence of the selected translators, especially Meng Ji, the Chinese MHLC Form C may be potentially insufficiently relevant, understandable, and acceptable in terms of the wordings and sentence structures of some items. Considering this possible insufficiency, we made a systematic comparison both between the two Chinese versions and between these two translated versions and the original English version, informed by Tang and Dixon (2002). Considering that the form can be purposefully changed to ensure equivalence of meaning (Sperber, 2004), we used some translation techniques including addition, deletion, substitution, omission, recasting, etc., therefore changing the form of the original text (Shan et al., 2023a, 2023b). We found these strategies effective in this study, contrary to the finding of Sperber (2004), who regarded these techniques as common translation errors. Through systematic comparisons and corresponding revisions, we effectively improved the cultural relevance, comprehensibility, and acceptability of the Chinese MHLC Form C.

In addition to the aforementioned methods of translation and adaptation, we used the approach of cognitive debriefing during testing the Chinese MHLC Form C with a small number of monolingual Chinese-speaking participants, which is imperative to validate the clarity and appropriateness (relevance) of the target-language version (Maneesriwongul & Dixon, 2004).

3.4.1.2 Efficacy Clusters and Associated Factors Identified

We identified 2 subgroups of patient participants, the low and moderate self-efficacy groups, which represented 72.5 and 27.5% of the total sample respectively. Patients in the low self-efficacy cluster (Cluster 1, 72.5%) had the following characteristics: (1) being less likely to believe in their own capability to achieve optimal outcomes in the prevention and treatment of depression; (2) having limited trust in medical and health professionals and the health benefits of adhering to their recommendations and advice; (3) having mixed views on the influence of others' behaviors on their own

3.4 Discussion

health; and (4) having mixed views on the role of luck in one's health management. Patients in the moderate self-efficacy cluster (Cluster 2, 27.5%) displayed distinct psychological traits. They had polarized views regarding the role of chance, internal motivations, and doctors in terms of the prevention and treatment of depression. All of them were more unlikely to associate their own depression outcomes with other people in their lives. In addition, we identified nine factors that were significantly associated with low self-efficacy, including (1) older age, (2) male sex, (3) limited educational attainment, (4) higher level of self-reported disease knowledge, (5) limited functional health literacy, (6) limited communicative health literacy, (7) limited critical health literacy, (8) limited digital health literacy, and (9) limited health numeracy literacy.

3.4.2 Implications

This study can provide some implications for clinical practice, health education, medical research, and public health policy-making. First, to translate scales for use in the target language and culture, rigorous translation and adaptation steps must be undertaken to ensure the cultural relevance, comprehensibility, and acceptability of the translated instruments. Translation is a challenging task, which calls for skill, knowledge, and experience (Sperber, 2004). Rigorous translation procedures, cultural nuances, jargon, idiomatic phrases, and emotionally evocative words (Sperber, 2004) all make the already challenging translation task even more complicated (Shan et al., 2023a, 2023b). To overcome these difficulties, we not merely carefully selected translators but also rigorously applied translation and adaptation strategies. As a result, we managed to successfully convey the original meanings and intents by choosing culturally equivalent linguistic expressions (Sperber, 2004), which were largely relevant, understandable, and acceptable to Chinese readers in the Chinese cultural contexts.

The two self-efficacy clusters and nine factors contributing to low self-efficacy can serve as important indicators for screening male patients with low self-efficacy to deliver more targeted education and more effective interventions to enhance their self-efficacy. Knowledge, skills, beliefs, and practices associated with the low self-efficacy class and the contributing factors could be integrated into public health education about and interventions in health beliefs about bladder cancer prevention and treatment among male patients to enhance their self-efficacy. Medical researchers can gain some insights into the topic of low self-efficacy and the contributing factors. Informed by this study, they could identify patients with low self-efficacy among their ethnic and socioeconomic groups, verify the contributing factors ascertained in this study, and find more contributors in future studies. Finally, our research results and findings can provide some implications for public health policy-making in the future.

3.4.3 Limitations

This study has some limitations. First, we did not test the internal consistency and test–retest reliability of the newly-developed Chinese MHLC Form C, although we used it to classify patient participants into two clusters. In future studies, we need to validate its reliability before applying it for other research purposes. Second, the generalizability of our research results and findings may be limited. The recruitment of patients from only one hospital was most likely to make the results and findings less generalizable to populations in other provinces in China and to patients in different linguistic and cultural communities worldwide. Further research is warranted to validate the results and findings among populations of diverse ethnic and sociocultural backgrounds. Third, the self-reported nature of the collected data may result in some bias. As claimed in Van der Varrt et al. (2011), self-reported literacy skills are not necessarily consistent with the actual abilities to comprehend, utilize, and appraise online health information. More objective measures need to be developed to increase the reliability and consistency of assessment of various health literacy and health beliefs and self confidence among culturally and linguistically diverse people. Finally, comparison could not sufficiently be made with previous studies due to the scarcity of relevant literature. Hopefully, our study can attract close attention from researchers, who can further examine this topic to add to the body of literature and expand knowledge, which could promote academic conversation around such a topic of social significance.

3.4.4 Conclusions

We used the depression-specific Chinese version to classify the patient participants into different latent classes according to their attitudes towards and beliefs about the prevention and treatment of depression, and identified significant factors that were closely associated with the low-efficacy cluster to provide essential implications for the delivery of tailored education and interventions and the administration of targeted prevention and treatment. After rigorous translation and adaptation procedures, we developed a culturally relevant, understandable, and acceptable Chinese MHLC Form C that is depression specific. Using this newly developed scale, we identified two subgroups defined as the low and moderate self-efficacy clusters which represented 72.5 and 27.5% of the total sample respectively. Patients in the low self-efficacy cluster (Cluster 1, 72.5%) had the following characteristics: (1) being less likely to believe in their own capability to achieve optimal outcomes in the prevention and treatment of depression; (2) having limited trust in medical and health professionals and the health benefits of adhering to their recommendations and advice; (3) having mixed views on the influence of others' behaviors on their own health; and (4) having mixed views on the role of luck in one's health management. Patients in the moderate self-efficacy cluster (Cluster 2, 27.5%) displayed distinct psychological traits. They had polarized views regarding the role of chance, internal motivations, and doctors in terms of the prevention and treatment of depression. All of them were more unlikely to associate their own depression outcomes with other people in their lives. In addition, we identified nine factors that were significantly associated with low self-efficacy, including (1) older age, (2) male sex, (3) limited educational attainment, (4) higher level of self-reported disease knowledge, (5) limited functional health literacy, (6) limited communicative health literacy, (7) limited critical health literacy, (8) limited digital health literacy, and (9) limited health numeracy literacy. This was the first study that investigated the attitudes towards and beliefs about the prevention and treatment of depression among patients in mainland China. Given the rising prevalence of the depressive disorder worldwide and in mainland China in recent years, the low self-efficacy cluster and associated contributing factors identified in this study can provide essential implications for clinical practice, health education, medical research, and health policymaking.

Abbreviations

LOC	Locus of control
AAHLS	The All Aspects of Health Literacy Scale
eHEALS	The eHealth Literacy Scale
MHLC	The Multidimensional Health Locus of Control (MHLC) Scales
COHL	The communicative health literacy scale of the AAHLS

References

ALL ASPECTS OF HEALTH LITERACY SCALE (AAHLS). https://healthliteracy.bu.edu/documents/34/AAHLS%20Tool.pdf. Accessed 26 June, 2022.

Bane, C., Hughes, C. M., & McElnay, J. C. (2006). The impact of depressive symptoms and psychosocial factors on medication adherence in cardiovascular disease. *Patient Education and Counseling, 60*(2), 187–193.

Barger, B., Nabi, R., & Hong, L. Y. (2010). Standard back-translation procedures may not capture proper emotion concepts: A case study of Chinese disgust terms. *Emotion, 10*(5), 703–711.

Barros, A., Santos, H., Moreira, L., & Santos-Silva, F. (2022). Translation and cross-cultural adaptation of the cancer health literacy test for Portuguese cancer patients: A pre-test. *International Journal of Environmental Research and Public Health, 19*(10), 6237.

Beaton, D. E., Bombardier, C., Guillemin, F., & Ferraz, M. B. (2000). Guidelines for the process of cross-cultural adaptation of self-report measures. *Spine, 25*(24), 3186–3191.

Berkman, N. D., Sheridan, S. L., Donahue, K. E., Halpern, D. J., & Crotty, K. (2011). Low health literacy and health outcomes: An updated systematic review. *Annals of Internal Medicine, 155*(2), 97–107.

Black, A. K. (2018). Language translation for mental health materials: a comparison of current back-translation and skoposthoerie-based methods. *All Theses and Dissertations*, 6720.

Brislin, R. W. (1970). Back-translation for cross-cultural research. *Journal of Cross-Cultural Psychology, 1*, 185–216.

Brislin, R. W., Lonner, W. J., & Thorndike, R. M. (1973). Questionnaire wording and translation. *Cross-cultural research methods* (pp. 32–58). John Wiley.

Brislin, R. W. (1980). Cross-cultural research methods. In I. Altman, A. Rapoport, & F. F. Wohlwill (Eds.), *Environment and culture* (pp. 47–82). Springer.

Chinn, D., & McCarthy, C. (2013). All Aspects of Health Literacy Scale (AAHLS): Developing a tool to measure functional, communicative and critical health literacy in primary healthcare settings. *Patient Education and Counseling, 90*, 247–253.

Donovan, D. M., & O'Leary, M. R. (1978). The drinking-related locus of control scale reliability, factor structure and validity. *Journal of Studies on Alcohol, 39*, 759–784.

Evans-Lacko, S., Aguilar-Gaxiola, S., Al-Hamzawi, A., et al. (2018). Socio-economic variations in the mental health treatment gap for people with anxiety, mood, and substance use disorders: Results from the WHO World Mental Health (WMH) surveys. *Psychological Medicine, 48*(9), 1560–1571.

Gebhardt, W. A., van der Doef, M. P., & Paul, L. B. (2001). The Revised Health Hardiness Inventory (RRHI-24): Psychometric properties and relationship with self-reported health and health behavior in two Dutch samples. *Health Education Research, 16*, 579–592.

Green, J. M., Coupland, A., & Kitzenger, S. (1990). Expectations, experiences and psychological outcomes of childbirth: A prospective study of 825 women. *Birth, 17*, 15–24.

Hilton, A., & Skrutkowski, M. (2002). Translating instruments into other languages: Development and testing processes. *Cancer Nursing, 25*(1), 1–7.

Institute of Health Metrics and Evaluation. Global Health Data Exchange (GHDx). https://vizhub.healthdata.org/gbd-results/. Accessed March 4, 2023.

Jääskeliänien, R. (2010). Think-aloud protocol. In Y. Gambier & L. van Doorslaer (Eds.), *Handbook of translation studies* (pp. 371–373). John Benjamins Publishing Co.

Johnson, J. L., & Cameron, M. C. (2001). Barriers to providing effective mental health services to American Indians. *Mental Health Services Research, 3*(4), 215–223.

Jomeen, J., & Martin, C. (2002). The impact of clinical management type on maternal and neo-natal outcome following pre-labour rupture of membranes at term. *Clin Effective Nursing, 6*(1), 3–9.

Jones, E. G., & Kay, M. (1992). Instrumentation in cross-cultural research. *Nursing Research, 41*(3), 186–188.

Koo, M., Norman, C., & Chang, H. M. (2012). Psychometric evaluation of a Chinese version of the eHealth Literacy Scale (eHEALS) in school age children. *International Journal of Health Education, 15*, 29–36.

Lavender, T., Walkinshaw, S. A., & Walton, J. (1999). A prospective study of women's views of factors contributing to a positive birth experience. *Midwifery, 15*, 40–46.

Lewis, F. M., Morisky, D. E., & Flynn, B. S. (1978). A test of the construct validity of health locus of control: Effects on self-reported compliance for hypertensive patients. *Health Education Monographs, 6*, 138–148.

Macleod, L., & Macleod, G. (1998). Control cognitions and psychological disturbance in people with contrasting physically disabling conditions. *Disability and Rehabilitation, 20*, 448–456.

Maneesriwongul, W., & Dixon, J. K. (2004). Instrument translation process: A methods review. *Journal of Advanced Nursing, 48*(2), 175–186.

Martin, N. J., Holroyd, K. A., & Penzien, D. B. (1990). The headache-specific locus of control scale: Adaptation to recurrent headaches. *Headache, 30*, 729–734.

Martin, C. R. (1999). Phasic influences on psychometric measures during the menstrual cycle: Implications for the construct integrity of the locus of control dimension. *British Journal of Medical Psychology, 72*, 217–226.

Martin, C. R., & Jomeen, J. (2004). The impact of clinical management type on maternal locus of control in pregnant women with pre-labour rupture of membranes at term. *Health Psychol Update, 13*, 3–13.

Morgan, G. (2014). Mixed mode latent class analysis: An examination of fit index performance for classification. *Structural Equation Model Multidisciplinary J, 22*(1), 76–86.

Morovati, D. (2014). *The intersection of sample size, number of indicators, and class enumeration in LCA: A Monte Carlo study*. University of California.

Nazareth, M., Richards, J., Javalkar, K., Haberman, C., Zhong, Y., Rak, E., et al. (2016). Relating health locus of control to health care use, adherence, and transition readiness among youths with chronic conditions, North Carolina, 2015. *Preventing Chronic Disease, 13*, 160046.

Nylund-Gibson, K., & Choi, A. Y. (2018). Ten frequently asked questions about latent class analysis. *Translational Issues Psychological Sci, 4*(4), 440–461.

Nutbeam, D. (2000). Health literacy as a public health goal: A challenge for contemporary health education and communication strategies into the 21st century. *Health Promotion International, 15*(3), 259–267.

Pang, S. K., Ip, W. Y., & Chang, A. M. (2001). Psychosocial correlates of fluid compliance among Chinese haemodialysis patients. *Journal of Advanced Nursing, 35*, 691–698.

Pastor, M. A., Salas, E., Lopez, S., Rodriguez, J., Sanchez, S., & Pascual, E. (1993). Patients' beliefs about their lack of pain control in primary fibromyalgia syndrome. *British Journal of Rheumatology, 32*, 484–489.

Saltzer, E. B. (1982). The weight locus of control (WLOC) scale: A specific measure for obesity research. *Journal of Personality Assessment, 46*, 620–628.

Sarafino, E. P. (2006). *Health psychology: Biopsychosocial interactions*. Wiley.

Scott-Palmer, J., & Skevington, S. M. (1981). Pain during childbirth and menstruation: A study of locus of control. *Journal of Psychosomatic Research, 25*, 151–155.

Shan, Y., & Ji, M. (2023). The Chinese version of the breast cancer literacy assessment tool: Translation, adaptation, and validation study. *JMIR Formative Research, 7*, e43002.

Shan, Y., Ji, M., Dong, Z., Xing, Z., & Xu, X. (2023a). Assessing patients' critical health literacy and identifying associated factors: Cross-sectional study. *Journal of Medical Internet Research, 25*, e43342.

Shan, Y., Xing, Z., Dong, Z., Ji, M., Wang, D., & Cao, X. (2023b). Translating and adapting the DISCERN instrument into a simplified Chinese version and validating its reliability: Development and usability study. *Journal of Medical Internet Research, 25*, e40733.

Sousa, V. D., Hartman, S. W., Miller, E. H., & Carroll, M. A. (2009). New measures of diabetes self-care agency, diabetes self-efficacy, and diabetes self-management for insulin-treated individuals with type 2 diabetes. *Journal of Clinical Nursing, 18*(9), 1305–1312.

Sousa, V. D., & Rojjanasrirat, W. (2011). Translation, adaptation and validation of instruments or scales for use in cross-cultural health care research: A clear and user-friendly guideline. *Journal of Evaluation in Clinical Practice, 17*, 268–274.

Sperber, A. D. (2004). Translation and validation of study instruments for cross-cultural research. *Gastroenterol, 126*(Suppl 1), S124–S128.

Strudler-Wallston, B., & Wallston, K. A. (1978). Locus of control and health: A review of literature. *Health Education Monograph, 6*, 107–117.

Takaki J, & Yano E. (2006). Possible gender differences in the relationships of self-efficacy and the internal locus of control with compliance in hemodialysis patients. *Behavioral Medicine, 32*(1):5–11.

Tang, S. T., & Dixon, J. (2002). Instrument translation and evaluation of equivalence and psychometric properties: The Chinese sense of coherence scale. *Journal of Nursing Measurement, 10*(1), 59–76.

Tein, J., Coxe, S., & Cham, H. (2013). Statistical power to detect the correct number of classes in latent profile analysis. *Structural Equation Modeling: A Multidisciplinary Journal, 20*(4), 640–657.

The General Health Numeracy Test (GHNT-6). https://healthliteracy.bu.edu/documents/36/GHNT_6%20.pdf. Accessed 26 June, 2022.

Tinsley, B. J., Trupin, S. R., Owens, L., & Boyum, L. A. (1993). The significance of women's pregnancy-related locus of control beliefs for adherence to recommended prenatal health regimens and pregnancy outcomes. *Journal of Reproductive and Infant Psychology, 11*, 97–102.

Ubbiali, A., Donati, D., Chiorri, C., Bregani, V., Cattaneo, E., Maffei, C., & Visintini, R. (2008). The usefulness of the Multidimensional Health Locus of Control Form C (MHLC-C) for HIV+ subjects: An Italian study. *AIDS Care: Psychological and Socio-Medical Aspects of AIDS/HIV, 20*(4), 495–502. https://doi.org/10.1080/09540120701867115

Van der Vaart, R., Van Deursen, A., Drossaert, C. et al. (2011). Does the eHealth literacy scale (eHEALS) measure what it intends to measure? Validation of a Dutch version of the eHEALS in two adult populations. *Journal of Medical Internet Research, 13*(4): e86.

Wallston, B. S., Wallston, K. A., Kaplan, G. D., & Maides, S. A. (1976). Development and validation of the health locus of control (HLC) scale. *Journal of Consulting and Clinical Psychology, 44*, 580–585.

Wallston, K. A., Wallston, B. S., & DeVellis, R. (1978). Development of the Multidimensional Health Locus of Control (MHLC) scales. *Health Education Monographs, 6*, 161–170.

Wallston, K. A., Stein, M. J., & Smith, C. A. (1994). Form C of MHLC scales: A condition-specific measure of locus of control. *Journal of Personality Assessment, 63*(3), 534–553.

World Health Organization. Depressive disorder (depression). March 31, 2023. https://www.who.int/news-room/fact-sheets/detail/depression

Woody, C. A., Ferrari, A. J., Siskind, D. J., Whiteford, H. A., & Harris, M. G. (2017). A systematic review and meta-regression of the prevalence and incidence of perinatal depression. *Journal of Affective Disorders, 219*, 86–92.

Zeugfang, D., Wisetborisut, A., Angkurawaranon, C., Aramrattana, A., Wensing, M., Szecsenyi, J., et al. (2018). Translation and validation of the PACIC+ questionnaire: The Thai version. *BMC Family Practice, 19*, 123.

Open Access This chapter is licensed under the terms of the Creative Commons Attribution-NonCommercial-NoDerivatives 4.0 International License (http://creativecommons.org/licenses/by-nc-nd/4.0/), which permits any noncommercial use, sharing, distribution and reproduction in any medium or format, as long as you give appropriate credit to the original author(s) and the source, provide a link to the Creative Commons license and indicate if you modified the licensed material. You do not have permission under this license to share adapted material derived from this chapter or parts of it.

The images or other third party material in this chapter are included in the chapter's Creative Commons license, unless indicated otherwise in a credit line to the material. If material is not included in the chapter's Creative Commons license and your intended use is not permitted by statutory regulation or exceeds the permitted use, you will need to obtain permission directly from the copyright holder.

Chapter 4
Development of a Method and an Assessment Construct for Person-Centered Translation of Dementia Public Stigma Scales

Abstract There are almost no available methods and assessment constructs for person-centered translation of dementia public stigma scales. This study aims to develop such a method and such an assessment construct by translating the Dementia Public Stigma Scale (DPSS) into Chinese. We translated the DPSS following three major steps: (1) literal translation and mistranslation identification; (2) panel discussions of items with problematic translations; and (3) the final checking of the translated scale. Informed by the translation and adaptation process, we then developed a method for person-centered translation of dementia public stigma scales. Based on this method and our panel discussions, we finally proposed a three-item assessment construct for the quality evaluation of the translation of dementia public stigma scales. Forward and backward translation did not work sufficiently in dementia public stigma scale translation. Mistranslations were induced by three major causes, including confusion caused by multiple Chinese meanings of the immediate Chinese direct translation, the lack of immediate Chinese direct translation because of varying positive/negative emotions attached to multiple translations, and the lack of culture-specific idioms in Chinese. Based on these factors, we proposed a three-item dementia translation assessment construct. Following this assessment tool, we determined the best Chinese version that could be further tested for its psychometric properties among the public. A method and an assessment construct for person-centered translation of dementia public stigma scales were developed. Such a method and such an assessment construct could be followed in the translation and translation evaluation of dementia public stigma scales.

Keywords Development · Method · Assessment construct · Person-centered translation · Dementia public stigma scale

4.1 Introduction

4.1.1 Prevalence of Dementia and Dementia-Related Stigma

With the number of people with dementia dramatically increasing over time (Wu et al., 2018), dementia is regarded as a major health concern worldwide (Prince et al., 2013). About 50 million individuals are currently diagnosed with dementia globally and without a medical breakthrough, this is projected to rise to 131.5 million by 2050 (Prince et al., 2015). Of this amount, an apparently-increasing proportion will be identified in Latin America, Africa, India, China, South Asia, and the Western Pacific region (Department of Economic and Social Affairs, Population Division, 2013). The number of people living with dementia in China has been estimated to be 9.5 million in the population aged 60 years or older (Wu et al., 2018). Despite the high prevalence and growing trend of dementia in China, this disease is conceptualized as a stigmatized mental disorder in contemporary Chinese society (Zhang, 2018). In the Chinese context of cultural, social, and political undesirabilities characterizing such a condition, there is increased stigmatization of such a mental condition in this country (Zhang, 2018). The increased public awareness that the mind constitutes a key concern in maintaining a high quality of life in contemporary China reinforces the persistence of dementia-related stigma in the public, which manifests itself in the form of silencing, indifference, or ignorance in memory clinics or other public settings (Zhang, 2018). In this background of research, it is imperative to provide a scale assessing dementia public stigma in China to deliver targeted education and interventions and launch dementia stigma reduction initiatives.

Growing evidence has shown that dementia is regarded as one of the most feared health conditions (Alzheimer's Association, 2014). Some people with dementia experience social stigma (Herrmann et al., 2018) caused by fear and lack of public awareness and understanding of dementia (Mukadam & Livingston, 2012). Dementia-related stigma brings about a potential barrier to care and support (Burgener et al., 2015a, 2015b) that can manifest itself in such behaviors as excluding individuals with dementia in healthcare decisions (Brannelly, 2011) or shunning family members of individuals living with dementia (Werner et al., 2011). However, there is limited research focusing on dementia stigma and few evidence-based interventions specifically targeting dementia stigma (Werner et al., 2012). The public health influence of reducing dementia stigma can contribute to better care access, greater support engagement, and ultimately higher life quality for individuals with dementia and their families (Goffman, 1986).

4.1.2 Stigma as a Social Construct

Stigma is a perspective "generated in social contexts" (Goffman, 1986: 138), where a socially salient group difference is identified, devalued, and used as a source of discrimination against individuals or groups (Corrigan & Watson, 2002). Stigma consists mainly of public stigma (a negative reaction to a stigmatized individual or group from non-stigmatized others), affiliated stigma (the experience of stigma in individuals associated with a stigmatized person), and self stigma (the negative attitudes that a stigmatized person perceives from society and internalizes in himself or herself) (Corrigan & Watson, 2002). As observed by Corrigan and Watson, public stigma underpins affiliated stigma and self stigma (Jones & Corrigan, 2014). Based on this observation, we believe that it is imperative to study public stigma before examining affiliated and self stigma.

Stigma has been widely viewed as a social construct in the literature. Goffman regards stigma as "spoiled identity," a gap between "virtual social identity" (how a person is characterized by society) and "actual social identity" (the attributes actually possessed by a person) (Goffman, 1986: 2). As such, the stigmatizing process is relational: the social environment defines what is deviant and provides the context where devaluing evaluations are expressed (Jones 1984). According to the Modified Labeling Theory, stigma is a social construct in which powerful groups in society impose negative stereotypical labels on those who are deemed undesirable and subsequently devalued and subjected to discrimination (Link & Phelan, 2001). Crocker et al. (1998) also define stigma socially. They claim that stigma occurs when a person is believed to possess an "often objective" characteristic conveying a particular devalued social identity in a specific social context (Crocker et al., 1998). Such an identity is socially constructed by defining who belongs to a specific social group and whether an attribute will lead to a given devalued social identity in a particular social context (Yang et al., 2007). Like Goffman (1986), Crocker et al. define stigmas as an essentially "devaluing social identity" that occurs within a particular social context that defines a feature as devaluing (Crocker et al., 1998: 505). Since stigma is socially constructed and dependent on relationship and context (Major & O'Brien, 2005), the sociocultural environment where stigma occurs (Link & Phelan, 2001) and the myriad societal forces that shape exclusion from social life (Parker & Aggleton, 2003) need to be considered in stigma-related studies. This is true for studies on dementia-related stigma. Considering the sophistication of stigma as a complex social construct, we think it advisable to explore public stigma before investigating affiliated and self stigma when it comes to a particular mental condition like dementia.

4.1.3 Developing Socioculturally-Relevant Dementia Public Stigma Scales

The relevance of worldwide translation and study of dementia public stigma

Despite the high prevalence of 131.5 million individuals living with dementia worldwide by 2050 (Prince et al., 2013), negative attitudes towards and discrimination against people with dementia are quite common (Batsch & Mittelman, 2012;

O'Connor et al., 2018). Given the wide-ranging consequences of dementia-related stigma, such as low self-esteem, poor psychological well-being, social isolation, and poor quality of life (Kim et al., 2022), it is imperative to develop psychometrically sound scales to measure this stigma. Such instruments are essential for providing knowledge about how to develop interventions for dementia-related stigma reduction in the community (Kim et al., 2022).

Some dementia stigma scales have been developed. Stigma questionnaire (Cheng et al., 2011), STIG-MA (Piver et al., 2013), and Dementia Stigma Questionnaire (Woo & Chung, 2013) were adapted from multiple sources, and their construct validity has not been tested to allow for capturing the complexity of stigma. These instruments have, therefore, been rarely adopted till now (Kim et al., 2022). The validated Family Stigma in Alzheimer's Disease Scale reflects three main dimensions of family stigma (caregiver stigma, lay public stigma, and structural stigma) (Werner et al., 2011). It was designed to assess family members' perceptions of the stigma held by the public rather than lay public attitudes towards people living with Alzheimer's disease (Kim et al., 2022). The validated Dementia Attitudes Scale (O'Connor & McFadden, 2010) assesses people's positive attitudes to people with dementia rather than common stereotypes or negative attitudes towards dementia and people with dementia (Kim et al., 2022). It is also not designed to measure structural discrimination or perceived personhood (e.g., enjoying life and interaction) that might be regarded as an essential aspect of dementia stigma underlying and impacting individual stigmatizing attitudes and behaviors (Stites et al., 2018). To better capture dementia public stigma, stereotypes of people with dementia, such as being dangerous (Cohen et al., 2009), being a burden to family and the health care system, being incapable of speaking for themselves, being unreliable, and being unable to contribute to the society (Werner et al., 2017), need to be covered in dementia public stigma scales. To this end, Kim et al. (2022) developed and validated the Dementia Public Stigma Scale (DPSS) which comprises the three components of the tripartite model of stigma (cognitive, emotional, and behavioral) (Corrigan, 2000; Pachankis, 2007) to assess dementia-related stigma in the public. Based on the theoretical model of Attribution Theory (Corrigan, 2000), the DPSS can facilitate understanding the formative factors underpinning stigma and allow for a more nuanced exploration of dementia stigma and its impacts across or within populations. To our knowledge based on the literature review, it is the latest and most systematic scale for assessing dementia public stigma.

Though comprehensive, valid, and reliable in the Australian sociocultural context, the DPSS may not be completely applicable to other sociocultural contexts, considering that there is no accepted "gold standard" for assessing dementia-related stigma (Herrmann et al., 2018) as stigma is a complex social construct shaped by the sociocultural environment (Link & Phelan, 2001) and various social forces (Parker & Aggleton, 2003). As such, it is relevant to translate and adapt the DPSS and other systematic scales, if any, to diverse languages and cultures and study dementia public stigma in these linguistic-cultural contexts for intervention purposes.

4.1 Introduction

Developing a method and an assessment construct for the translation of dementia public stigma scales by translating the DPSS into Chinese

Herrmann et al. (2018) reviewed worldwide evidence on dementia stigma over the past decade, focusing on how stigmatizing attitudes may present themselves in various ethnic subgroups, stigma assessment instruments, and prospective or experimental approaches to stigma assessment and management. As they discovered, only one cross-sectional study was conducted by Cheng and colleagues in China (Herrmann et al., 2018). Cheng et al. found lower levels of stigma in participants with relatives or friends living with dementia and younger and more educated individuals (Cheng et al., 2011) using 11 English assessment items derived from other stigma scales (Taylor & Dear, 1981; Fife & Wright., 2000; Struening et al., 2001; Mak et al., 2007). The assessment tool they developed through synthesizing diverse currently-available evaluation instruments may, to some extent, be neither sufficiently systematic in assessment nor adequately relevant to the target sociocultural context. A scale appropriate to the Chinese language and culture is needed to exclusively assess dementia public stigma among Chinese populations.

The recently developed DPSS was designed to measure dementia-related public stigma in the general public, and its psychometric properties were initially evaluated with community-dwelling adults (Kim et al., 2022). This scale is a 5-factor, 16-item construct. The five factors are Fear and Discomfort (Items 1–4), Incapability (Items 5–9), Personhood (Items 10–12), Burden (Items 13–14), and Exclusion (Items 15–16). Responses to the 16 items are measured through a seven-point Likert scale ranging from 1 (strongly disagree) to 7 (strongly agree). The total scores achievable for this tool, therefore, vary from 16 to 112. Six items are reverse-scored (1, 2, 3, 10, 11, and 12). As regards the other items, a higher score indicates a more negative attitude towards dementia. The DPSS displayed moderate to high reliability in all five factors (Cronbach's $\alpha = 0.805$ for Factor 1, 0.738 for Factor 2, 0.743 for Factor 3, 0.796 for Factor 4, and 0.743 for Factor 5). The whole scale also showed high reliability (Cronbach's $\alpha = 0.818$). Item analysis also indicated that removing any of the 16 items would not increase Cronbach's Alpha value. Capturing the cognitive, emotional, and behavioral domains of stigma, the DPSS can explore the factor structure underpinning dementia pubic stigma among the study participants (Kim et al., 2022).

Based on our analysis of the studies reported by Herrmann et al. (2018), particularly Cheng et al. (2011), the dementia-related expertise of four authors (Lee-Fay Low, Sarang Kim, Annica Barcenilla-Wong, and Sam Shen) of our study, and our consultations with some mental health professionals working at the Hospital Affiliated with Nantong University and Qilu Hospital of Shandong University, we believed that the brief, user-friendly, and quick-to-complete assessment instrument of the DPSS could reveal dementia public stigma in the Chinese sociocultural context if well translated and adapted to the Chinese language and culture. Currently, there is no available dementia public stigma scale developed in Chinese to adopt targeted approaches to countering or eliminating dementia-related stigma, including protest, education, and contact (Rüsch et al., 2005). Protest is meant to fight against stigmatizing public statements, media reports, and advertisements; education is designed to reduce stigma by conveying contradictory information through books, videos, structured teaching programs, and other forms; contact with those with mental illness is intended to increase the impacts of education on decreasing stereotypes and mental health stigma (Rüsch et al., 2005). In this context, translating already-developed tools for use is a rapid and practical approach to assessment (Chang et al., 2014) before delivering more tailored stigma-mitigating interventions or launching more targeted stigma-reducing initiatives.

Given painstaking efforts as well as considerable time and cost investments involved in developing new instruments (Chang et al., 2014), well-developed, available, and reliable instruments need to be adapted and validated cross-linguistically (Mohamad Marzuki et al., 2018; Zhao et al., 2022). As such, there is a pressing need to translate quantitative scales into the language of the culture in which these tools are adopted (Maneesriwongul & Dixon, 2004). Strategies need to be used in the whole translation and adaptation process to ensure semantic equivalence and cultural appropriateness, including "forward translation, semantics evaluation and consolidation of the translated version, back translation, translation equivalence testing, and further adaptation" (Shan et al., 2023). Based primarily on the forward–backward translation approach, these strategies could basically guarantee that an instrument is adapted in "a culturally relevant and comprehensible form" without changing its original meaning and intent (Sperber, 2004). Such strategies are informative and helpful for the translation of the original English version of the Dementia Public Stigma Scale. This is especially true when we consider the different lexical systems, different language registers, and distinct cultural expression repertoires between the source and target languages and cultures. To ensure a successful translation of this scale and help develop a dementia public stigma reduction initiative (Herrmann et al., 2018) in China, we aimed to develop a person-centered translation method that could produce culturally-acceptable dementia public stigma scales by achieving semantic closeness and accuracy and cultural relevance and to develop an assessment construct for evaluating the translation of dementia public stigma scales.

4.2 Design and Methods

4.2.1 Overall Design

First, we translated and adapted the DPSS following three major steps. Informed by the translation and adaptation process, we then developed a method for person-centered translation of dementia public stigma scales. Based on this method and our panel discussions during translation and adaptation, we finally proposed a three-item assessment construct for the quality evaluation of the translation of dementia public stigma scales.

4.2 Design and Methods

4.2.2 Developing the Chinese Version of the DPSS

Drawing on and developing the methodologies adopted in previous studies (Maneesriwongul & Dixon, 2004; Shan et al., 2023; Sperber, 2004; Guillemin et al., 1993; Sousa & Rojjanasrirat., 2011; Sidani et al., 2010), we developed the Chinese version of the DPSS following three major steps below.

1. First, we literally translated the DPSS into Chinese.
2. A panel comprising bilingual health educators, bilingual translators, the scale author, and content experts met to discuss items with problematic translations and corresponding root causes by double-checking the target version against the source version. Discussion of the meaning of the items and possible translations was undertaken until consensus was obtained. An adapted English item was sometimes written in conjunction with the Chinese translation. The consequences of forced literal translation and their implications for translation were also worked out through panel discussion.
3. The final translated scale was sent back to all panel members for checking.

4.2.3 Developing a Method and an Assessment Construct for Person-Centered Translation of Dementia Public Stigma Scales

The development of a method and an assessment construct for person-centered translation of dementia public stigma scales was informed conceptually by the translation and adaptation guidelines reported in relevant studies (Guillemin et al., 1993; Maneesriwongul & Dixon, 2004; Shan et al., 2023; Sidani et al., 2010; Sousa & Rojjanasrirat., 2011; Sperber, 2004) and practically by the accumulated health translation experience of three authors of this study (Meng Ji, Yi Shan, and Weiwei Chu) and the translation process above. Thus informed, we focused on penal discussions after literal translation, making full use of the potential advantages of the panel members: the language proficiency of native Chinese speakers (Meng Ji, Yi Shan, and Weiwei Chu) and native English speakers (Lee-Fay Low, Sarang Kim, Annica Barcenilla-Wong, and Sam Shen); the health translation experience of bilingual translators (Meng Ji, Yi Shan, and Weiwei Chu); and the expertise of the scale author of the DPSS (Sarang Kim) and content experts (Lee-Fay Low, Annica Barcenilla-Wong, and Sam Shen) who are engaging in studies on mental health with a special focus on dementia. Such penal discussions ensured not only the linguistic appropriateness and comprehensibility and cultural relevance and accessibility of the translated scale but also the maintenance of the original meaning and intent of the source scale (Shan et al., 2023). The method developed was presented schematically in the Results section. Based on this method and our panel discussions, we finally proposed a three-item assessment construct for the quality evaluation of the translations of dementia public stigma scales, which was also provided in the Results section.

Kim proposed a people-centered theory of translation by advocating a focus on "what people need, what people can do and what people think and feel" (Kim, 2009: 258) in translation. Informed by this proposal, we tentatively developed a person-centered translation of dementia public stigma scales by mainly considering the dignity and self-esteem of persons with dementia and showing understanding of and sympathy for them from multiple perspectives of the health translators, the DPSS author, and dementia experts who well understand persons with dementia. We were thus concerned to uphold the personhood of people with dementia and cater to linguacultural appropriateness and relevance in the Chinese sociocultural context while maintaining the original meaning and intent of the DPSS when we addressed mistranslations and agreed upon the final Chinese version of the DPSS. We also put forth the three items of evaluation from the perspective of persons with dementia when proposing the assessment construct. Overall, such a person-centered orientation was implemented throughout the entire process of our study.

4.3 Results

The method for the person-centered translation of dementia public stigma scales we developed could be displayed schematically in Fig. 4.1. Revolving around this schematic diagram, we presented the results of this study in the following subsections.

4.3.1 Mistranslations Arising from the Literal Translation

We found the literal translation of Items 1, 2, 5, 9, and 16 problematic. Table 4.1 shows the specific literal translations and meanings of the literal translations of these items. It can be seen that the problems lay in the multiple meanings of the literal translation of "feel confident" in Item 1 and "touching" in Item 2, the possibilities of translating "supervise" in Item 5 and "ignore" in Item 16 into different Chinese phrases that have diverse meanings, and the lack of matching sayings in Chinese for "no longer themselves" in Item 9.

4.3.2 Root Causes of Mistranslations, Implications for Translation, and Consequences of Forced Literal Translations

The three factors identified as causes of the aforementioned mistranslations included: (1) The immediate Chinese direct translation can cause confusion because it has

4.3 Results

Fig. 4.1 Method for person-centered translation of dementia public stigma scales

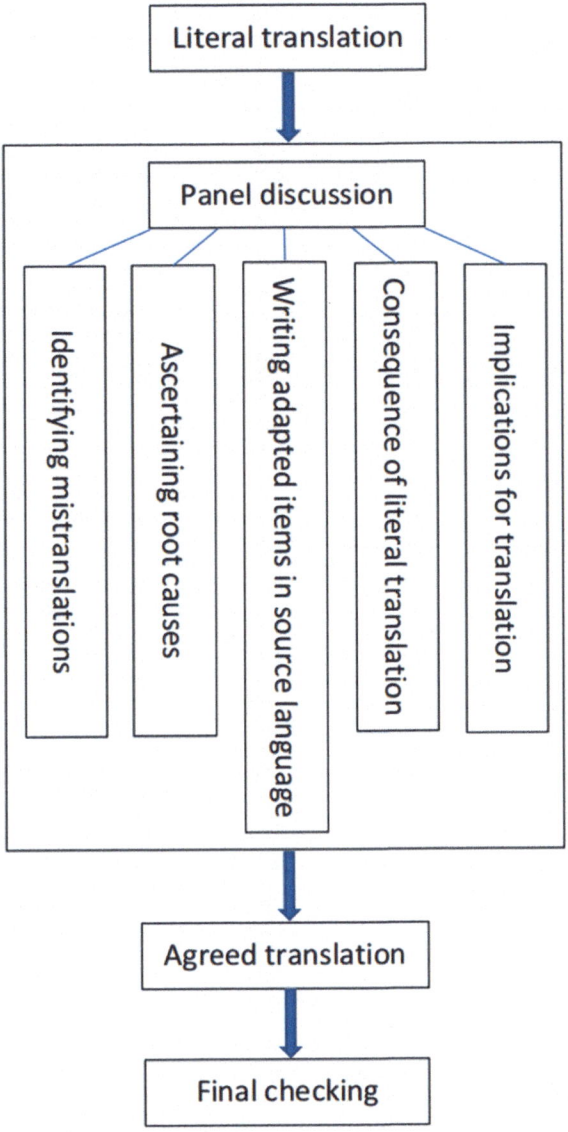

multiple Chinese meanings; (2) There is no immediate Chinese direct translation—multiple translations are possible with varying positive/negative emotions attached; and (3) There is the lack of counterpart culture-specific idioms in Chinese. In the final analysis, what underlay these three causes were three root causes, as listed in Table 4.2. Each of these root causes could provide an essential implication for translation, as shown in Table 4.2. Regardless of these implications, forced literal translations would incur severe consequences for the readers, as reported in Table 4.2.

Table 4.1 Mistranslations of Items 1, 2, 5, 9, and 16

Problematic items	Original English phrasing	Literal translation	Meaning of the literal translation in Chinese culture
Item 1	Feel confident	信心 (Xìnxīn)	A feeling of trust (in someone or something)
			A state of confident hopefulness that events will be favorable
			Any cognitive content held as true
			Belief in yourself and your abilities
			A strong belief in a supernatural power or powers that control human destiny
Item 2	Touching	接触 (Jiēchù)	Deal with
			Close interaction
			Perceive via the tactile sense
			Come in contact with
			In physical contact
Item 5	Supervise	管理	The act of managing something—(neutral)
		看管	Keep tabs on, keep an eye on (slightly negative, informal language: adults to children)
		监督	Watch and direct, oversee (moderately negative, formal language: authorities to individuals)
		监视	Keep under surveillance, monitor (strongly negative)
Item 16	Ignore	忽视	The trait of neglecting responsibilities and lacking concern
		漠视	Willful lack of care and attention, disregard
		不理睬	Fail to acknowledge, give little or no attention to
		轻视	Treat with contemptuous disregard
		冷遇	A refusal to recognize someone you know
		蔑视	Look down on with disdain
		排斥	Marginalize, relegate to a lower or outer edge, as of specific groups of people
Item 9	No longer themselves	No matching sayings in Chinese	

It follows that the forward–backward translation method proposed in previous studies (Guillemin et al., 1993; Maneesriwongul & Dixon, 2004; Shan et al., 2023; Sidani et al., 2010; Sousa & Rojjanasrirat, 2011; Sperber, 2004) did not work effectively in dementia stigma scale translation.

4.3 Results

Table 4.2 Root causes of mistranslations, Implications for translation, and consequences of forced literal translations

	Root causes	Implications for translation	Consequences of forced literal translations
1	English and Chinese have different lexical systems	One-to-one linear lexical matching is impossible since two large scenarios have been captured in our study: • One English word was translated into one Chinese word with multiple meanings (see Questions 1, 2) which could cause potential confusion • One English was translated to multiple competing words with distinct emotional and cultural connotations (see Questions 5, 16) that could stigmatize dementia	Misunderstanding and confusion to readers
2	Language registers (formality, abstractness) are different for health information in English and Chinese	Adapting English formal expressions to more natural, informal Chinese words	Lowered cultural believability, trustworthiness, and communicative effectiveness to readers
3	Cultural expression repertoires in two cultures are distinct	Using cultural equivalents in the target language to carry over the meaning (see Question 9, "people with dementia are no longer themselves"—changed to "changed into a different person")	Meaningless translation to readers

4.3.3 An Assessment Construct for Person-Centered Translation of Dementia Public Stigma Scales Proposed

Based on the analysis above, we proposed a construct that could facilitate translating the DPSS into Chinese, as shown in Fig. 4.2. This construct consists of three components: semantic meaning closeness (SMC), perceived cultural familiarity (PCF), and perceived psychological harms (PPH). It could be used as a model to guide the assessment of the Chinese translation of dementia stigma scales.

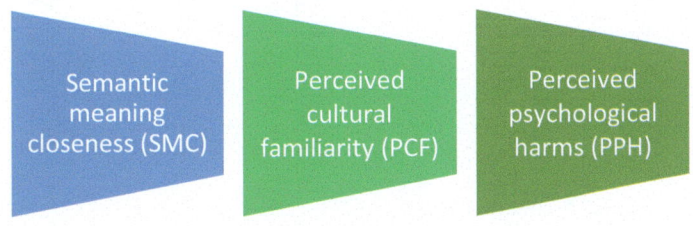

Fig. 4.2 Assessment construct for the translation of dementia public stigma scales

4.3.4 Identification of the Best Translation Among Various Translation Options

Table 4.3 illustrates how our research team arrived at an agreed Chinese version of the DPSS before testing it for public use. A translated version was subjected to assessment in light of the three components comprising the construct shown in Fig. 4.2. As can be seen from this table, we conducted six rounds of translation before finally agreeing on the best version of translation that satisfied these three components. During the repeated translating processes, we managed to achieve semantic meaning closeness to the English wordings of "feel confident" in Item 1 and "touching" in Item 2 by avoiding such possible literal translations as listed in Table 4.1. Similarly, we avoided using such Chinese phrases with diverse negative meanings listed in Table 4.1 when translating "supervise" in Item 5 and "ignore" in Item 16. Translating "supervised" and "ignore" into "被人看管着" (watched over) and "躲开" (avoid) respectively could ensure accuracy in the meaning that we conveyed through the translation and meanwhile possibly prevent perceived psychological harm to target readers. As "are no longer themselves" in Item 9 has no corresponding culture-specific idioms in Chinese, we rendered it into a neutral wording of "好像变了一个人" (appear to become another person). The final Chinese version is shown in Table 4.4.

Table 4.3 Dementia public stigma scale translation assessment

Translation variants	Semantic meaning closeness to the English words (SMC)	Perceived cultural familiarity/acceptability to target readers (PCF)	Perceived psychological harm to target readers (PPH)
Explanations	How close is the meaning of the translation to the English word? There is no 100% matching translation to an English word, so literal translation is impossible in most cases, but we can strive to get the closest meaning in Chinese as possible	Is this translation the most natural way to convey the meaning? The translation cannot be too formal or too vulgar, which will reduce the cultural trust, affinity, and acceptability of the translation	Does the translation have strong negative connotations that would stigmatize a disease?
1	Yes	No	No
2	No	No	Yes
3	Yes	No	Yes
4	No	Yes	Yes
5	Yes	Yes	No
6	**Yes**	**Yes**	**Yes**

4.3 Results

Table 4.4 The final Chinese version of the DPSS

Question items	强烈反对 (SD)[a]	反对 (D)	稍微反对 (MD)	既不赞同也不反对 (Neutral)	稍微赞同 (MA)	赞同 (A)	非常赞同 (SA)
Q1 我知道在得了痴呆症的人身边应该怎么做。 I know how to behave around people with dementia	○	○	○	○	○	○	○
Q2 当触碰得了痴呆症的人，我不会感到任何不适。 When I physically touch people with dementia, I will not feel any discomfort	○	○	○	○	○	○	○
Q3 在得了痴呆症的人的身边，我还是感到一样轻松、自然。 When alongside people with dementia, I feel natural and at ease	○	○	○	○	○	○	○
Q4 我害怕那些得了痴呆症的人。 I am afraid of people with dementia	○	○	○	○	○	○	○
Q5 得了痴呆症的人应该总是被人看管着。 People with dementia should always be watched over	○	○	○	○	○	○	○
Q6 得了痴呆症的人行为和言语都不好预测。 The behavior and words of people with dementia are not easily predictable	○	○	○	○	○	○	○
Q7 得了痴呆症的人很像孩子一样。 People with dementia are very much like children	○	○	○	○	○	○	○
Q8 得了痴呆症的人无法做任何个人决定。 People with dementia cannot make any personal decision	○	○	○	○	○	○	○
Q9 得了痴呆症的人得了这个病之后就像变了一个人。 People with dementia appear to be another person after they have got this illness	○	○	○	○	○	○	○
Q10 得了痴呆症的人也可以享受生活 People with dementia may also enjoy life	○	○	○	○	○	○	○

(continued)

Table 4.4 (continued)

Question items	强烈反对 (SD)[a]	反对 (D)	稍微反对 (MD)	既不赞同也不反对 (Neutral)	稍微赞同 (MA)	赞同 (A)	非常赞同 (SA)
Q11 得了痴呆症的人也能够感受到别人对他们的关爱。 People with dementia may also feel the kindness from other people	○	○	○	○	○	○	○
Q12 和得了痴呆症的人很好地互动,这也是有可能的。 Having good interactions with people with dementia is possible	○	○	○	○	○	○	○
Q13 得了痴呆症的人对他们的家人来说是一种负担。 People with dementia are for their family a burden	○	○	○	○	○	○	○
Q14 得了痴呆症的人对医疗系统来说是一种负担。 People with dementia are for the healthcare system a burden	○	○	○	○	○	○	○
Q15 我不会让得了痴呆症的人参加各种活动。 I will not permit people with dementia to participate in different activities	○	○	○	○	○	○	○
Q16 我会躲开得了痴呆症的人。 I will avoid people with dementia	○	○	○	○	○	○	○

[a] SD = Strongly Disagree; D = Disagree; MD = moderately disagree; Neutral = not disagree nor agree; MA = moderately agree, A = agree; SA = strongly agree

4.4 Discussion

We tentatively developed a method for person-centered translation of dementia public stigma scales in this study. The translator needs to discuss the meaning of the original text with someone with content knowledge to avoid misinterpretations and optimize word choice when there are multiple possible translations. To this end, we proposed an assessment construct for the translation of dementia public stigma scales that incorporates three major components: semantic meaning closeness (SMC), perceived cultural familiarity (PCF), and perceived psychological harms (PPH). Such a construct could help minimize mistranslations involved in the translation of dementia public stigma scales due to the differences in lexical systems, language registers, and cultural expression repertoires between the source and target languages. It can be used as a guide to help health translators navigate the translation of dementia public stigma scales. Translations following the method and the assessment construct we developed could facilitate understanding and measuring dementia public stigma.

4.4 Discussion

We found that the forward and backward translation method did not work effectively in the translation of the DPSS into Chinese, detrimental to the understanding and measurement of dementia public stigma. Chang et al. (2014), Zhao et al. (2022), Mohamad et al. (2018), Maneesriwongul and Dixon (2004), Shan et al. (2023), Sperber (2004), Guillemin et al. (1993), Sousa and Rojjanasrirat (2011), Sidani et al. (2010), among many others, adopted forward and backward translation to adapt the English versions of some health-related measures into different languages. Although they concluded that this method was effective in their studies, we found it insufficient in our study. English and Chinese have different lexical systems, language registers, and cultural expression repertoires, which challenged the English-to-Chinese translation of the DPSS. These differences made it extremely difficult to forward-translate this scale into Chinese. For example, if "ignore" in Item 16 were forward-translated into "忽视" (the trait of neglecting responsibilities and lacking concern), "漠视" (willful lack of care and attention, disregard), "不理睬" (fail to acknowledge, give little or no attention to), "轻视" (treat with contemptuous disregard), "冷遇" (a refusal to recognize someone you know), "蔑视" (look down on with disdain), or "排斥" (marginalize, relegate to a lower or outer edge, as of specific groups of people), different degrees of discrimination or negative emotions would be induced, which is not intended in the original English scale. These translations would naturally lead to misleading backward translations, making translation equivalence testing (Shan et al., 2023; Sperber, 2004) considerably challenging. Translations thus produced could not effectively explore the cognitive, emotional, and behavioral domains of stigma held by the general public, therefore failing to gain a better understanding of dementia public stigma. Besides, the DPSS was written in a dementia-friendly language, in response to the appeal of Alzheimer's Australia (Alzheimer's Australia, 2009) in Dementia Friendly Language Position Paper 4, which advocates that "Language is a powerful tool" and "The words we use can strongly influence how others treat or view people with dementia." Considering this appeal, we believed that the forward and backward translation method would possibly distort the original meaning and intent of the DPSS, bringing additional stigma to individuals with dementia. As a result, such translated scales could not objectively solicit and measure public attitudes towards people with dementia. As "a true translation proceeds by the motions of understanding and sympathy" (Hoffman, 1991: 211), a health translator needs to keep "constantly examining the relationship between word and experience, i.e. signifier and signified" (Kim, 2009). To this end in our translation process, we attached great importance not merely to "the relationship between word and experience" to achieve linguistic appropriateness and cultural relevance from the perspective of health translators but also to the understanding of and sympathy for those with dementia from the perspectives of the DPSS author and dementia content experts. It can be said that our translation team played a role of "a powerful agent for cultural change," and our translation functioned as "a bridge-building space between the source and the target" (Bassnett, 2002: 9–10). As a result, the dementia pubic stigma scale translation in our study could ensure a translated scale that could effectively measure dementia public stigma and facilitate our understanding of such stigma.

We proposed a better alternative, a method for person-centered translation of dementia public stigma scales, to reveal and measure such stigma more objectively. This method was effective in facilitating the translation of the DPSS in a culturally relevant and appropriate manner (Shan et al., 2023). It allowed us to use words friendly to people with dementia and their families, those that are "normal, inclusive, jargon-free, non-elitist, clear, straightforward, non-judgmental" (Swaffer, 2014), and those that center on the person rather than on the disease or the social care system (Swaffer, 2014). Such wording can avoid stripping individuals of their dignity and self-esteem, reinforcing inaccurate stereotypes, and heightening the fear and stigma surrounding dementia (Alzheimer's Australia, 2009). Translated scales using such wording are most likely to assess stereotypes, prejudice, and discrimination among the general population, revealing their generalized negative beliefs, negative emotional reactions to stereotypes, and negative behavioral reactions resulting from prejudice (Rüsch et al., 2005). Our protocol can, therefore, be seen as an initiative counteracting the prevalent phenomenon that inappropriate language used in the literature, the media, and the community creates wrong descriptions, prescriptions, misconceptions, and stigma of individuals with dementia (Swaffer, 2014). A good case in point is such derogatory, stigmatizing, and discriminatory words as "demented," "sufferers," "subjects," and "victims" used by most researchers and presenters at the 2014 Alzheimer's Disease International Conference (Swaffer, 2014). In the context that the language being used remains stigmatizing, negative, and disempowering (Devlin et al., 2007), there is a pressing need to use "inclusive non-offensive language that supports the whole person positively, rather than negative demeaning language that stigmatizes and separates us" (Swaffer, 2014). In this case, the protocol we proposed in this study can contribute to the promoted use of person-centered, dementia-friendly language, especially in the translation of dementia public stigma scales. Counteracting inaccurate stereotypes and the resulting prejudice and discrimination against dementia, translated scales using such language could help us understand and assess the public attitudes towards dementia in more objectively.

Our study also points to the need to construct a person-centered theory of translation (Kim, 2009) of dementia-related materials or in health care and medical domains in general. To this end, health translation studies should be taken away from purely linguistic and cultural analysis. Health translation in specific social and cultural circumstances needs to fulfill its expected social and cultural roles. As such, before engaging in translating health materials and constructing health translation theories, health translators and translation theorists should ask themselves the following question: "In whose terms, to which linguistic constituency, and in the name of what kind of intellectual authority does one translate?" (Liu, 1995). To answer this question, health translators and translation theorists need to adopt a person-centered approach advocated by Robinson (1991) and Hoffman (1991) to consider "what people need, what people can do and what people think and feel" (Kim, 2009). In the context of the prevalent social stigma attached to dementia and other mental diseases, health translators and translation theorists need to spare no efforts to center on people with dementia and their relatives in their translation practices and theory construction to "change views of and about people with dementia," "include them in the

4.4 Discussion

research and conversations about them" (Kim, 2009), and "remove the stigma which we hear of every day in dementia" (Kim, 2009). The language being used about individuals with dementia is a powerful tool (Anon, 2010) for inclusion, reducing stigma, and increasing education and awareness as the way forward in reducing stigma (Bartlett, 2014). Provided that a people-centered theory of translation in health care and medical domains can be established, the disadvantaged position of patients could be improved through dementia-friendly, inclusive, non-offensive language in the translated materials about dementia and other mental diseases to some extent. Such a translation theory is "true to life" (Kim, 2009). Such translation theories are urgently needed, especially when considering that "Language creates the particularly human kind of rapport, of being together, that we are in a conversation together." (Hughes et al., 2006).

To establish a person-centered theory of dementia translation, we need to highlight the importance of the translator's role, which has already been stressed by famous translation scholars such as Bassnett (2002), Robinson (1991), Lawrence Venuti (1995), and Snell-Hornby (1995). To be qualified in health and especially dementia translation, translators should be equipped with essential "literacies," which include the ability to understand "what people need, what people can do and what people think and feel" (Kim, 2009), in addition to bilingual and bicultural competences (Snell-Hornby, 1995). They also need to enhance translatability by focusing on practice and cognition (Kim, 2009) to make dementia translation "a humanizing process" (Robinson, 1991).

Strengths and Limitations

To develop a method and an assessment construct for person-centered translation of dementia public stigma scales, we formed a research team comprising bilingual health educators, bilingual translators, the scale author, and content experts. Such a composition could ensure the quality of translation from different perspectives of experts in relevant domains, especially considering the interdisciplinary nature of dementia translation. Another strength lay in the bilingual translators' experience in community-based health translation for many years. Their rich health translation practice could enable them to gain a keen, sensitive sense of cross-cultural and -lingual differences both from the perspective of language and from the perspective of health care. This is beneficial to ascertaining the key steps of the person-centered translation method and the core elements of the translation quality assessment construct we tried to develop. The translation method and the assessment construct we developed may be used as a guide to help navigate the translations of dementia public stigma scales that can be used to develop and evaluate interventions aimed at dementia public stigma reduction in the public.

To our knowledge, they are the first method and the first assessment construct for person-centered translation of dementia public stigma scales that have been developed. Without relevant studies for reference, our translation method and assessment construct may not be perfect. Their reliability and efficacy need to be validated in future studies. Their applicability to other dementia-related materials than dementia public stigma scales needs to be further attested. As stigma is a complex social construct and the DPSS was developed in English-speaking populations in Australia, the Chinese version of the DPSS we developed may not be perfectly specific to the Chinese language and culture although we made great efforts to adapt it linguistically and culturally. In future validation studies, we will constantly improve its content validity based on psychometric tests among Chinese populations with diverse demographic characteristics.

Conclusions

The translation method and the assessment construct we developed are designed for facilitating the person-centered translation of dementia public stigma scales. They can help health translators navigate dementia translation to destigmatize people with dementia and their relatives while maintaining the original meaning and intent of the source text in a culturally relevant and appropriate manner in the target text. The best Chinese version of the DPSS we translated could be used for further evaluation with the public to test its psychometric properties. The translation method and the assessment construct we developed could be further validated for their reliability and efficacy in dementia public stigma scale translation and dementia translation in general.

References

Alzheimer's Australia. (2009). *Dementia friendly language: Position paper 4.* http://www.fightdementia.org.au/dementia-friendly-language.aspx
Alzheimer's Association. (2014). Alzheimer's disease facts and figures. *Alzheimer's & Dementia, 10*(2), e47-92.
Anon. (2010). *Body language is a powerful communication tool.* Independent Online (South Africa).
Bartlett, R. (2014). The emergent modes of dementia activism. *Ageing and Society, 34*, 623–644.
Bassnett, S. (2002). *Translation studies.* Routledge.
Batsch, N. L., & Mittelman, M. S. (2012). *World Alzheimer Report 2012: Overcoming the stigma of dementia.* https://www.alzint.org/u/WorldAlzheimerReport2012.pdf
Brannelly, T. (2011). Sustaining citizenship: People with dementia and the phenomenon of social death. *Nursing Ethics, 18*, 662–671.
Burgener, S. C., Buckwalter, K., Perkhounkova, Y., et al. (2015a). Perceived stigma in persons with early-stage dementia: Longitudinal findings: Part 1. *Dementia (london), 14*, 589–608.
Burgener, S. C., Buckwalter, K., Perkhounkova, Y., et al. (2015b). The effects of perceived stigma on quality of life outcomes in persons with early-stage dementia: Longitudinal findings: Part 2. *Dementia (london), 14*, 609–632.
Chang, M. C., Chen, Y. C., Gau, B. S., & Tzeng, Y. T. (2014). Translation and validation of an instrument for measuring the suitability of health educational materials in Taiwan: Suitability assessment of materials. *The Journal of Nursing Research, 22*(1), 61–68.
Cheng, S. T., Lam, L. C. W., Chan, L. C. K., et al. (2011). The effects of exposure to scenarios about dementia on stigma and attitudes toward dementia care in a Chinese community. *International Psychogeriatrics, 23*, 1433–1441.
Cohen, M., Werner, P., & Azaiza, F. (2009). Emotional reactions of Arab lay persons to a person with Alzheimer's disease. *Aging & Mental Health, 13*(1), 31–37.

References

Corrigan, P. W. (2000). Mental health stigma as social attribution: Implications for research methods and attitude change. *Clinical Psychology: Science and Practice, 7*(1), 48–67. https://doi.org/10.1093/clipsy.7.1.48

Corrigan, P. W., & Watson, A. C. (2002). Understanding the impact of stigma on people with mental illness. *World Psychiatry, 1*(1), 16–20.

Crocker, J., Major, B., & Steele, C. (1998). Social stigma. In S. Fiske, D. Gilbert, & G. Lindzey (Eds.), *Handbook of social psychology* (pp. 504–553). McGraw-Hill.

Department of Economic and Social Affairs, & Division, P. (2013). *World population aging*. United Nations.

Devlin, E., MacAskill, S., & Stead, M. (2007). 'We're still the same people': Developing a mass media campaign to raise awareness and challenge the stigma of dementia. *International Journal of Nonprofit and Voluntary Sector Marketing, 12*, 47–58.

Fife, B. L., & Wright, E. R. (2000). The dimensionality of stigma: A comparison of its impact on the self of persons with HIV/AIDS and cancer. *Journal of Health and Social Behavior, 41*, 50–67.

Goffman, E. (1986). *Stigma: Notes on the management of spoiled identity*. Simon & Schuster (Original work published 1963).

Guillemin, F., Bombardier, C., & Beaton, D. (1993). Cross-cultural adaptation of health-related quality of life measures: Literature review and proposed guidelines. *Journal of Clinical Epidemiology, 46*(12), 1417–1432.

Herrmann, L. K., Welter, E., Leverenz, J., Lerner, A. J., Udelson, N., Kanetshy, C., & Sajatovic, M. (2018). A systematic review of dementia-related stigma research: Can we move the stigma dial? *The American Journal of Geriatric Psychiatry, 26*, 316–331.

Hoffman, E. (1991). *Lost in translation: A life in a new language*. Minerva.

Hughes, J., Louw, S., & Sabat, S. (2006). Seeing the whole. In J. Hughes, S. Louw, S. Sabat, & e-Kindle (Eds.), *Dementia: Mind, meaning, and the person* (p. 475). Oxford University Press, Inc.

Jones, E. E., Farina, A., Hastorf, A. H., Markus, H., Miller, D. T., & Scott, R. A. (1984). *Social stigma: The psychology of marked relationships*. Freeman.

Jones, N., & Corrigan, P. W. (2014). Understanding stigma. In P. W. Corrigan (Ed.), *The stigma of disease and disability: Understanding causes and overcoming injustices* (pp. 9–34). American Psychological Association.

Kim, S., Eccleston, C., Klekociuk, S., Cook, P. S., & Doherty, K. (2022). Development and psychometric evaluation of the Dementia Public Stigma Scale. *International Journal of Geriatrics and Psychiatry*, 1–9.

Kim, S.-H. (2009). Towards a people-centered theory of translation. *Perspectives: Studies in Translatology, 17*(4), 257–272.

Link, B. G., & Phelan, J. C. (2001). Conceptualizing stigma. *Annual Review of Sociology, 27*, 363–385.

Liu, L. H. (1995). *Translingual practice: Literature, national culture, and translated modernity China, 1900–1937*. Stanford University Press.

Major, B., & O'Brien, L. T. (2005). The social psychology of stigma. *Annual Review of Psychology, 56*, 393–421.

Mak, W. W. S., Poon, C. Y. M., Pun, L. Y. K., & Cheung, S. F. (2007). Meta-analysis of stigma and mental health. *Social Science & Medicine, 65*, 245–261.

Maneesriwongul, W., & Dixon, J. K. (2004). Instrument translation process: A methods review. *Journal of Advanced Nursing, 48*(2), 175–186.

Mohamad Marzuki, M. F., Yaacob, N. A., & Yaacob, N. M. (2018). Translation, cross-cultural adaptation, and validation of the Malay version of the system usability scale questionnaire for the assessment of mobile apps. *JMIR Human Factors, 5*(2), e10308.

Mukadam, N., & Livingston, G. (2012). Reducing the stigma associated with dementia: Approaches and goals. *Aging and Health, 8*(4), 377–386.

O'Connor, D., Mann, J., & Wiersma, E. (2018). Stigma, discrimination and agency: Diagnostic disclosure as an everyday practice shaping social citizenship. *Journal of Aging Studies, 44*, 45–51. https://doi.org/10.1016/j.jaging.2018.01.010

O'Connor, M. L., & McFadden, S. H. (2010). Development and psychometric validation of the dementia attitudes scales. *International Journal of Alzheimer's Disease*, 1–10.

Parker, P., & Aggleton, P. (2003). HIV and AIDS-related stigma and discrimination: A conceptual framework and implications for action. *Social Science & Medicine, 5*, 13–24.

Pachankis, J. E. (2007). The psychological implications of concealing a stigma: A cognitive–affective–behavioral model. *Psychological Bulletin, 133*(2), 328–345.

Piver, L. C., Nubukpo, P., Faure, A., Dumoitier, N., Couratier, P., & Clément, J. P. (2013). Describing perceived stigma against Alzheimer's disease in a general population in France: The STIGMA survey. *International Journal of Geriatric Psychiatry, 28*(9), 933–938.

Prince, M., Bryce, R., Albanese, E., Wimo, A., Ribeiro, W., & Ferri, C. P. (2013). The global prevalence of dementia: A systematic review and metaanalysis. *Alzheimer's & Dementia, 9*, 63-75.e2.

Prince, M., Wimo, A., Guerchet, M., Ali, G.-C., Wu, Y.-T., & Prina, M. (2015). *World Alzheimer Report 2015: The global impact of dementia. An analysis of prevalence, incidence, cost and trends.* https://www.alz.co.uk/research/WorldAlzheimerReport2015.pdf

Robinson, D. (1991). *The translator's turn.* Johns Hopkins University Press.

Rüsch, N., Angermeyer, M. C., & Corrigan, P. W. (2005). Mental illness stigma: Concepts, consequences, and initiatives to reduce stigma. *European Psychiatry, 20*, 529–539.

Shan, Y., Xing, Z., Dong, Z., Ji, M., Wang, D., & Cao, X. (2023). Translating and adapting the DISCERN instrument into a simplified Chinese version and validating its reliability: Development and usability study. *Journal of Medical Internet Research, 25*, e40733.

Sidani, S., Guruge, S., Miranda, J., Ford-Gilboe, M., & Varcoe, C. (2010). Cultural adaptation and translation of measures: An integrated method. *Research in Nursing & Health, 33*(2), 133–143.

Snell-Hornby, M. (1995). *Translation studies: An integrated approach.* John Benjamins.

Sousa, V. D., & Rojjanasrirat, W. (2011). Translation, adaptation and validation of instruments or scales for use in cross-cultural health care research: A clear and user-friendly guideline. *Journal of Evaluation in Clinical Practice, 17*(2), 268–274.

Sperber, A. D. (2004). Translation and validation of study instruments for cross-cultural research. *Gastroenterology, 126*(Suppl 1), S124–S128.

Stites, S. D., Rubrigh, J. D., & Karlawish, J. (2018). What features of stigma do the public most commonly attribute to Alzheimer's disease dementia? Results of a survey of the U.S. general public. *Alzheimer's Dement, 14*(7), 925–932.

Struening, E. L., et al. (2001). Stigma as a barrier to recovery: the extent to which caregivers believe most people devalue consumers and their families. *Psychiatric Services, 52*, 1633–1638.

Swaffer, K. (2014). Dementia: Stigma, language, and dementia-friendly. *Dementia, 13*(6), 709–716.

Taylor, S. M., & Dear, M. J. (1981). Scaling community attitudes toward the mentally ill. *Schizophrenia Bulletin, 7*, 225–240.

Venuti, L. (1995). *The translator's invisibility: A history of translation.* Routledge.

Werner, P., Goldstein, D., & Heinik, J. (2011). Development and validity of the Family Stigma in Alzheimer's Disease Scale (FS-ADS). *Alzheimer Disease and Associated Disorders, 25*(1), 42–48.

Werner, P., Goldstein, D., & Buchbinder, E. (2010). Subjective experience of family stigma as reported by children of Alzheimer's disease patients. *Qualitative Health Research, 20*, 159–169.

Werner, P., Mittelman, M. S., Goldstein, D., et al. (2012). Family stigma and caregiver burden in Alzheimer's disease. *Gerontologist, 52*, 89–97.

Werner, P., Jabel, H. A., Reuveni, Y., & Prilutzki, D. (2017). Stigmatic beliefs toward a person with Alzheimer's disease among high-school students: Does majority–minority status make a difference? *Educational Gerontology, 43*(12), 609–610.

References

Woo, B. K. P., & Chung, J. O. P. (2013). Public stigma associated with dementia in a Chinese-American immigrant population. *Journal of the American Geriatrics Society, 61*(10), 1832–1833.

Wu, Y. T., Ali, G. C., Guerchet, M., Prina, A. M., Chan, K. Y., Prince, M., & Brayne, C. (2018). Prevalence of dementia in mainland China, Hong Kong and Taiwan: An updated systematic review and meta-analysis. *International Journal of Epidemiology, 47*(3), 709–719.

Zhang, Y. (2018). Governing dementia: A historical investigation of the power of states and professionals in the conceptualization of dementia in China. *Culture, Medicine and Psychiatry, 42*, 862–892.

Zhao, S., Cao, Y., Cao, H., Liu, K., Lv, X., Zhang, J., et al. (2022). Chinese version of the mHealth app usability questionnaire: Cross-cultural adaptation and validation. *Frontiers in Psychology, 13*, 813309.

Yang, L. H., Kleinman, A., Link, B. G., Phelan, J. C., Lee, S., & Good, B. (2007). Culture and stigma: Adding moral experience to stigma theory. *Social Science & Medicine, 64*, 1624–1535.

Open Access This chapter is licensed under the terms of the Creative Commons Attribution-NonCommercial-NoDerivatives 4.0 International License (http://creativecommons.org/licenses/by-nc-nd/4.0/), which permits any noncommercial use, sharing, distribution and reproduction in any medium or format, as long as you give appropriate credit to the original author(s) and the source, provide a link to the Creative Commons license and indicate if you modified the licensed material. You do not have permission under this license to share adapted material derived from this chapter or parts of it.

The images or other third party material in this chapter are included in the chapter's Creative Commons license, unless indicated otherwise in a credit line to the material. If material is not included in the chapter's Creative Commons license and your intended use is not permitted by statutory regulation or exceeds the permitted use, you will need to obtain permission directly from the copyright holder.

SPRINGER NATURE

GPSR Compliance

The European Union's (EU) General Product Safety Regulation (GPSR) is a set of rules that requires consumer products to be safe and our obligations to ensure this.

If you have any concerns about our products, you can contact us on ProductSafety@springernature.com

In case Publisher is established outside the EU, the EU authorized representative is:

Springer Nature Customer Service Center GmbH
Europaplatz 3
69115 Heidelberg, Germany